MARKED!

The mark of the beast! What is it? Is it the Universal Product Code? Your Social Security number? World currency? Is it visible or invisible? Secular or religious? You owe it to yourself and your loved ones to learn the facts concerning a cosmic death struggle between supernatural beings!

BOB SPANGLER

Review and Herald Publishing Association
Washington, D.C. 20012

Edited by Raymond H. Woolsey
Book designed by Alan Forquer
Cover by Jeff Dever
Printed in U.S.A.

Library of Congress Cataloging in Publication Data

Spangler, Bob.
  Marked!
  1. Salvation. I. Title.
BT751.2.S63   234   81-8598
ISBN 0-8280-0079-4   AACR2

Printed in U.S.A.

CONTENTS

This book will
make more sense if you
read this first:

All of us—or most of us—are acquainted with jigsaw puzzles. Each piece of a puzzle has its own individuality in colors and shape, and could really have no perceptible meaning until it takes its own place and is fitted in to the entire picture. The chief difference between the concept of putting together a jigsaw puzzle and getting the most out of this book is that with a jigsaw puzzle there is no particular order in which you must put the pieces together. But this book on the mark of the beast does have a planned sequence. In fact, most books do! However, the nature of this subject usually creates such an interest that the reader wants to know immediately what the mark of the beast is! The problem is, you can't give an answer to that question in just a few words. This is why I have written an entire book on the subject. And the chapters are arranged in such a way as to lead your mind in a logical step-by-step understanding of what the mark is.

I am reminded of Francis Bacon who said, in essence, "Some books are to be tasted: others swallowed: and some few to be chewed and digested." This book fits, I believe, the latter category. So let me urge you not to skim through the book or to read the last chapters first, but rather to be systematic—begin at the very beginning and carefully go through it page by page.

It is my earnest hope that when you finish reading the book you will have come to grips with a concept that will bring not only enlightenment but a blessing to your soul. Each chapter is a piece in a spiritual jigsaw puzzle, but the pieces must be put together in proper sequence.

Even after you have finished reading this book, you will have only touched the surface of the grand themes of the mark of the beast and the seal of God. Therefore, to assist you in a continuing quest to explore further dimensions relating to this important subject, notice an advertisement on the last pages regarding a special offer. I urge you to avail yourself of the opportunity of systematizing your understanding of Biblical themes and their meaning in our time, by enrolling in a free-correspondence Bible course that is yours for the asking.

Above all else, remember that spiritual truths must be spiritually discerned. That means that we need the guidance of God's Holy Spirit to direct our minds in order for us to understand His ways and will. As you journey through this book from Chapter 1 through the last chapter, may you have a rich experience in the things of God.

Bob Spangler

Is
It Really
Important?

Is the Universal Product Code a forerunner of the "mark of the beast"? There are those who believe that the little black bars of varying width that have turned up in recent years on everything from cereal boxes to shoe polish containers are indeed part of an insidious plot to make it impossible to buy or sell without submitting to the "beast" and its "mark." Others see in laser beam technology a potential means of indelibly and painlessly marking every individual on earth with a code or number that would allow enforcement of the "mark of the beast." Indeed, such technology *is* already being used to identify animals, these believers point out.

Still others see veiled implications of the occult or of the mystic number 666 in corporate symbols of certain banks or manufacturing concerns. (Proctor and Gamble and an Australian financial conglomerate have been singled out recently.) A small cadre of influential conspirators (the Illuminati or the Trilateral Commission) biding their time before taking control of the world; blank identification cards stockpiled in Switzerland in sufficient numbers for every man, woman, and child on earth; a world currency, printed and awaiting distribution at the proper time; a plan for a unified world government presented prematurely at the United Nations and subsequently hushed up—each of these rumors has its staunch adherents regardless of the evidence or the lack thereof.

Such concerns are not the exclusive domain of the "lunatic fringe." Hollywood's interest in Satan, demon possession, antichrist, and the occult remains high. Ever since *The Exorcist* was released in 1974, a continuing lineup of similar movies—*Omen I* and *Omen II, The Shining, The Awakening*—have kept the subject before theatergoers. The popular science-fiction film thrillers of recent years—such as *Close Encounters of the Third Kind, Star Wars*—have raised the specter of nonhuman forces in the universe, both benevolent and malevolent, vitally interested in the affairs of earth.

At the same time, the catalogs of religious book publishers regularly offer new titles in this area, many of which attempt to identify the antichrist. (A former Secretary of State, long a prime suspect, seems to be losing ground due to his inactivity in government affairs the past few years.) Probably few periods of time have seen a greater interest on the part of Christian and non-Christian alike in the satanic and the occult.

Among Christians, especially conservative evangelicals, the conviction seems to be growing that the events mentioned in the book of Revelation regarding the end of the world, and conditions just prior to its end, are on the verge of fulfillment.

Meanwhile, the world situation—energy shortages threatening changed life styles, seemingly insurmountable inflation and economic uncertainty, shifting moral patterns, widespread use of drugs, a declining role for once-powerful nations—causes even the most confirmed skeptic in religious matters to think seriously about where man is headed. The result is an unprecedented concern and interest in the world's future and the role that supernatural forces may play.

All this has focused attention on a critical, if somewhat enigmatic, passage of Scripture—Revelation 14:6-12. Here John, a disciple of Jesus, describes three angels who fly through the air, each proclaiming a special message. The first angel issues a call to worship God, the Creator of all things. The second solemnly declares the fall of Babylon. The third heavenly messenger speaks of a "beast," and a "mark" that it causes men to receive. This third message also warns of extremely dire consequences to those who accept this "mark of the beast."

Since these three messages come at a very crucial point in John's narrative, let's take a moment to consider their context in order to understand them better. If we can see what John has been talking about both before and after these angels' words, we can see how they fit into the overall picture of the future that God gave him.

One of the keys to understanding the entire book of Revelation, and the messages of the three angels in particular, is to realize that this earth is the center of a great struggle going on between good and evil—between Christ and heaven on the one hand and Satan on the other. Each wants to have the allegiance of man and control of this earth, but for vastly different purposes. Christ wants to bring human beings back to their original perfection and happiness. Satan wants to impose his rule on men in order to continue and strengthen his rebellion against God. (We'll have more to say about Satan's rebellion and the beginning of sin in a later chapter.)

This theme of a continuing cosmic struggle between evil and good is one that runs all through the Bible and is especially prominent in the book of Revelation. This struggle is brought to its sharpest focus in the messages of the three angels. Here is made clear that it is a struggle in which we all have a part, for we must choose whether our allegiance shall go to Jesus Christ or to Satan. This contrast is presented in terms of receiving a "mark of the beast" (which, as we will see, is the agent of Satan), or receiving the "seal of God." (See Revelation 7.)

Do you begin to see the great importance of these messages and why God is so concerned about those who accept the mark of the beast? It is not nearly so important for us to speculate about what the mark might consist of or how it might be applied as it is to realize that it represents apostasy from God and acceptance of all that is opposed to truth, righteousness, and love.

In contrast to the great multitudes that will turn from God to worship the beast, John, who records the vision of the three angels, saw a group who by God's grace stand firm against evil and are delivered from the power of the beast (see Rev. 14:1-5). Notice the unique spiritual experience of this group. They have the "Father's name written in their foreheads" (verse 1). Those who turn from God to accept the beast receive its mark in their forehead; those faithful to God carry His name, or seal, in theirs (see chap. 7:2-4). This contrast between the "mark of the beast" and the "seal of God" is of vital importance and is a theme that runs through the entire messages given by the three angels.

Immediately following his description of the three angels' messages, John pictures the glorious second coming of Jesus to earth from heaven (chap. 14:14-20). So the three angels and their messages apply to the current time—the last days of earth just before Jesus comes. They are given during the climactic events leading up to the coming of Jesus. That is why they are so important. They constitute God's final message to the world—His last invitation and appeal to men and women to place themselves on the side of right against the dragon and the beast. Thus the mark of the beast will be clearly identifiable in the final hours of earth's history that lie just before us. While the principles of the mark of the beast and the seal of God have always existed, individuals receive the actual mark only when the test of loyalty to God is made clear just prior to the return of Jesus Christ.

It is certain, then, that there will be only two groups when Jesus comes: those who worship Him and receive His seal, and those who worship the beast and receive its mark. The three angels' messages are a plea for faithfulness in the face of mounting persecution and apostasy.

I believe these words of God are of the utmost

importance to every human being on earth today. But it is not my purpose in this book to identify the "beast" or "antichrist" with any current world figure or to determine whether lasers will be used to etch a mark in people's hands or foreheads. I will not be dealing in sensational speculations regarding the future, nor will I try to unravel the mysterious 666, said to be the number of the beast.

Instead, I will focus in this book on what God's Word has to say about the beast and its mark in the context of the three angels' messages in which they are mentioned. I will try to make plain what significance these ancient messages have for life today in the twentieth century—and they *do* have significance! I will seek to answer why God pronounces on the beast, and on those who worship it and receive its mark, the most severe and relentless doom, unmitigated with mercy, to be found anywhere in the Bible. Above all, I will attempt to demonstrate that, though couched in the negative language of warning, these solemn words spoken by flying angels are not primarily messages of destruction and God's wrath; rather, rightly understood, they speak to us of salvation and God's undying love for the inhabitants of earth.

Man,
the Marvel

As a lad, I would sometimes look at a dog and wonder, "Why was I born a boy instead of a dog?" Or I would look at another person and wonder, "Why am I me and not him?"

Later I went through the interesting stage of wondering whether my parents were really mine, or was I an adopted child? My older sister used to tease me about being adopted, but a comparison of my nose with my father's comforted me. We both had the Spangler nose, a rather prominent identifying feature! Those childhood experiences of questioning have long passed. I have no doubts, now, of who I am or where I came from.

A close friend from college days told me that she had not learned that she was adopted until she was a teen-ager. She had an identical twin sister, of whom she had known absolutely nothing. Hers was a remarkable story of intrigue and heartache as she attempted to uncover her past. The supreme moment of excitement came when both sisters, dressed in identical clothes, left their respective homes, and took trains to the same city. They met each other for the first time in the station and put an **X** on the floor where they embraced. Each thought she was looking into a mirror when she saw the other, so alike were they. It was a never-to-be-forgotten experience.

In recent years a rather interesting phenomenon has come about that can be summed up with one word—*roots*. Alex Haley's book by that title became a best-seller and a renowned attraction on television. Haley tells the story of the search for his own family roots, which eventually led him to a small African village, the home of his ancestors. Many today are interested in uncovering their roots and learning of their ancestors. But what about our real "roots"? Where did man come from?

Unless we fully grasp the implications of who we are and where we came from, the mark of the beast—and its counterpart, the seal of God—cannot be totally understood. The Scriptures are clear and unequivocal regarding our origin. Genesis 1:27 says simply, yet profoundly: "God created man in his own image." This theme of God as man's Creator is repeated throughout the Scriptures. The last book of the Old Testament asks, "Have we not all one Father? hath not one God created us?" (Mal. 2:10). Jesus Himself referred to man's grand beginning in these words: "'At the beginning the Creator made them male and female'" (Matt. 19:4, N.I.V.). The apostle Paul, addressing Greeks in Athens, declared, "God . . . hath made of one blood all nations of men. . . . For we are also his offspring" (Acts 17:24-28).

"God created man in his *own image.*" What does that say to us? It says that man was created perfect! If man was made in God's image, he had to be perfect!

Anything created in the image or likeness of God can be nothing less than perfect! Dr. Luke brings his genealogical record to a thrilling climax with the words, "the son of Adam, the son of God" (Luke 3:38, N.I.V.). Adam was the son of God, a perfect, noble, well-balanced being, a person whose holy thoughts and righteous actions brought honor to God and blessing to himself. This is man's true beginning. We are rooted in God Himself! No more elevated and noble origin can be imagined. Nothing can surpass it. It should inspire and motivate our every thought and action.

"But," you ask, "doesn't the theory of evolution present a different concept?" Yes. But remember that the idea that man developed through a process of evolution is only hypothesis. It is *not* a fact that can be demonstrated or proved any more than can the Biblical story of Creation. Both require a leap of faith to believe. In my opinion, it requires a much smaller leap of faith to believe the Bible story than to believe the evolutionary story.

Some Christians attempt to harmonize the evolutionary theory with the Biblical record by teaching that the evolutionary process is God's method of creating, but the Scriptures do not support the idea that man developed from a lower form of life to a higher one over a long period of time, either with or without God. In fact, the very opposite is clearly taught in the first chapter of the first book of the Bible. The record there sets forth six days of creative activity by God, climaxed by a seventh day of rest, later called the Sabbath. God knew that someday His creative power would be challenged. So He inspired the author of Genesis to repeat after each of the six days of Creation, "and the evening and the morning were the first [second, third, et cetera] day." Thus He clearly indicated that the first week of earth's time was composed of seven literal days, and not long ages measured by millions or billions of years.

Furthermore, God placed in the heart of the Ten Commandments the fourth commandment, which distinctly commands man to honor as sacred the seventh-day Sabbath, because "in six days the Lord made heaven and earth, the sea, and all that in them is, and rested the seventh day" (Ex. 20:11).

In the light of this command it simply does not make sense to consider these days anything more or less than regular twenty-four-hour days, composed of a dark and light part like any other day. Try to substitute the term "billion years" for "day" in the fourth commandment, and you can see how utterly senseless it sounds: "In six billion years the Lord made heaven and earth, the sea, and all that in them is, and rested the seventh billion years." If this were the correct interpretation of the fourth commandment, you can easily perceive how ridiculous the rest of the commandment would be: "Six billion years shalt thou labour, and do all thy work; but the seventh billion years are the sabbath of the Lord thy God. In them thou shalt not do any work." How meaningless for God to give such a command to man, whose life span is measured in mere decades.

Thus Genesis, taken at face value, gives the simple, factual account of man's origin. "Then the

Lord God formed man of dust from the ground, and breathed into his nostrils the breath of life; and man became a living being" (Gen. 2:7, R.S.V.). King Solomon, one of the world's wisest men, declared that "God made man upright" (Eccl. 7:29, R.S.V.). Again we find that man's original condition as he came from the creating hand of God was one of uprightness, which in this particular text means *to be right*, or *righteous*.

Mankind, therefore, is the crowning act of God's creation. Even the Greek philosopher Sophocles commented, "There are many wonderful things in nature, but the most wonderful of all is man." Thousands of years ago King David asked the important question, "What is man?" The inspired answer points to God's exalted intentions for us. "What is man that you are mindful of him, the son of man that you care for him? You made him a little lower than the heavenly beings and crowned him with glory and honor" (Ps. 8:4, 5, N.I.V.). The Hebrew word for "heavenly beings" in this text can be translated "God," according to the footnote. In other words, our ancestry is impeccable. All of us, by creation, are sons and daughters of the universe's Supreme Ruler! Royal blood flows through our veins! Sublime, almost unbelievable, the thought that you and I were created in the image of the omnipotent God! If only we fully sensed our divine ancestry, our lofty lineage, our affiliation with God, the royal Progenitor of us all, what a difference it would make not only in our attitude toward ourselves but in our attitude toward God and toward others!

MARKED!

Man is not merely a two-legged animal; he is not, as Mark Twain said, "the only animal that blushes. Or needs to." He is not "a great mischievous baboon," as Dr. William Harvey, discoverer of the human circulatory system, called him. Rather, man is a special, unique creation of God. We do not exist accidentally; we are the product of God's love, thought, design, and power.

What gratification and joy this brings us! But with it comes a corresponding responsibility to live worthy of our heritage. A lad of common birth may do certain things and live in a way that a son of the king cannot. Likewise, if we forget or ignore our regal origin, we make a far greater ruin than would those who had no such grand potential at the start. And this is precisely why we find ourselves today so degraded from our original position. A tragedy has taken place—the tragedy of the ages—as we will see in the next chapter.

Man,
the Failure

My seatmate on a jetliner bound for Washington, D.C., from Chicago was a young university student working on an advanced degree in the area of the causes and solutions of juvenile delinquency. During most of the seventy-five-minute flight, he gave a glowing report of his classwork and field projects. I finally was able to interrupt and ask, "What success are you having in actually changing the life styles of the delinquents you work with?" His reponse was a look of dismay that seemed to say, "Why did you have to ask *that* question?" Grudgingly he admitted, "To be quite honest, none of our field projects are making much headway in changing these kids' behavior." Then I asked (although I knew the answer), "In any of your classes do you study what the Scriptures have to say about the nature of man?"

"Of course not!" he retorted. "I'm not attending a religious school!"

"I know," I replied. "But I want to make a point that can spell the difference between success and failure in your working with youth who are in trouble." This awakened enough interest so that he was willing to listen, and for the next few minutes I took the

MARKED!

Scriptures and unfolded to him what God says about the nature of man. When we landed, this secular-minded young intellectual said, "I am not a Christian, but what you have told me from the Bible makes more sense than anything I've ever heard about why people act the way they do."

Some of what I shared from God's Word with that young student you will find in this chapter. The previous chapter concluded with the thought that something happened to man that could be described as the tragedy of the ages.

Originally, man was created perfect. He had no disposition or desire to sin. He was happy and content to obey God and to enjoy life to the very fullest. He had not the slightest inclination toward thinking or doing evil. But one day tragedy struck, and a radical change occurred in man's nature. If you find it difficult to accept the Biblical account of what happened to mankind, remember that the mother of every mur-derer, alcoholic, rapist, and thief has found it utterly impossible to believe that that tiny, precious baby she cuddled so lovingly in her arms could eventually end up as he did. If sweet, innocent infants, reared by caring parents in a wholesome environment, can terminate their lives on death row of the penitentiary, don't think it strange that Adam and Eve fell into sin and rebellion in spite of starting life with a flawless nature and in immaculate surroundings.

In a definite sense their sin placed them and their offspring in a global "death row." What I am talking about is man's degeneracy from a sinless nature to a sinful nature, and as a result, his falling under the death penalty. According to the Bible, this is exactly what happened.

Of course, we don't like to think of man (and ourselves in particular) as having a sinful nature even from birth. We would much rather contemplate the high and noble state of our first parents as they stood in their perfection following their creation in God's image. But the Scriptures unequivocally teach that man has so far left his original perfection that everyone is born with an inherent sinful nature.

What does the term "sinful nature" mean? As C. S. Lewis points out in *Mere Christianity*,* there is what every society in history has termed "right" and "wrong." In my own brief life span I have visited countries on every continent of earth, and as I have observed and questioned people everywhere, I find it amazing that there is such common agreement on what is right and wrong. I have yet to find a society—whether it be in Borneo or Britain, Japan or Jamaica—that endorsed and praised murderers, thieves, rapists, or liars. Of course, some individuals do these things and feel no apparent remorse or shame, but society in general does not approve of them. So there is a rather commonly held, worldwide sense of right and wrong, even among uncivilized tribes. The human race seems to have a deep-seated conviction that there is a certain standard of behavior that everyone ought to go by. If they do so, they are right, and if they don't, they are wrong. In other words, by nature man has a certain limited sense of which actions are right and which are wrong.

Of Gentiles—those who did not believe in God or

23

His revealed will in Scriptures and who were not privileged, as were the Hebrews, to know right and wrong specifically from a God-given law—the apostle Paul says, "Indeed, when Gentiles, who do not have the law, do by nature things required by law, they are a law for themselves, even though they do not have the law, since they show that the requirements of the law are written on their hearts, their consciences also bearing witness, and their thoughts now accusing, now even defending them" (Rom. 2:14, 15, N.I.V.). Paul is describing not illiterates only but also the well-educated and intellectual, yet godless, people.

The point is that people by nature have consciences, and to a degree they have inherent ideas of right and wrong. Yet, left to themselves, they can know right and wrong only in a limited way. Their inherent concepts of morality are usually confined to those standards that affect relationships with others. God-oriented areas, such as idolatry and Sabbathkeeping, in which people must be taught what is right and wrong, do not come naturally!

There is another important aspect of this concept. Even though the human race by nature knows the rightness and wrongness of certain actions, we all know also that we fall far short of obeying those standards. Every one of us has had, or perhaps has even now, a terrible sense of guilt for our actions. A mother, frustrated with a child, loses her temper and beats him unmercifully. A man hurls a nasty remark at someone in the office who seems to have better rapport with the boss than he does. A bank teller overpays when cashing a check, and the payee does not return the money. A secretary uses office stamps for personal use. A husband has a secret affair with a girl he met at a club. Why does man, who claims to believe in a code of morality, proceed to violate that code? We find a remarkably uniform acceptance around the world and in all kinds of societies of certain standards for acceptable behavior. Yet we find an equally uniform failure to follow those standards.

The Bible tells us the reason. The previous chapter set forth at some length the fact that God made mankind perfect, with absolutely no bent toward evil. God made man in His own image, with capacities to think, love, serve, and obey. Adam and Eve in their original sinless state found their highest joy in obedience to the loving Creator. But because they had a nature akin to God's, they were given the power of choice—the power not only to obey but the power to *disobey* as well. God in His magnificent love created them with this freedom to choose.

Notice how important this quality of choice really is. If we had no choice, at best we would be like the animals or even like inanimate objects such as a machine, a star, a planet, a flower, or a rock. It is true that a star cannot disobey the rules set down for its existence by its Creator, but how happy is a star? How much gratitude and love can it experience? The sense of love exists only among those who have the power of choice. How much real love would a wife have for her husband if she were merely programmed like a computer to show affection but was without the freedom to choose to love him of her own free will?

God gave us this freedom in order for us to *choose*

to love Him. He knows such freedom of choice is the only basis on which love can exist. Obedience can be forced, but not love. Through the centuries various religions have used force in an attempt to produce acceptance and love. But love that is coerced is not love at all. Thousands have waved aloft their burning fingers in persecution's fires because they refused to be forced into believing and accepting some religious concept.

Furthermore, if people had no choice, there could be no growth in love or in their understanding of God. If they did not have the ability to steal—no capacity or possibility of choosing to steal—they could never really understand honesty. If they had no possibility of being sexually immoral, the idea of purity and morality would be meaningless to them. Thus the qualities that make life truly human—love, loyalty, honesty, purity, integrity, et cetera—would be unknowable and unexperienced. Life could never be truly lived, but only endured. Man would merely exist. He could never experience the joy of serving his Creator because he wanted to do so.

Thank God, He did not make us that way. Of course, once He gave us the freedom to choose, He ran the terrible risk that we would make wrong choices, but better to run that risk than to create us merely on the level of animals or things. He already had plenty of these in His universe. No need for more. We were designed to be different, to be in His own image.

You see, God wanted to create beings who could be His companions, beings with whom He could share

His love. The first several chapters of Genesis give us this insight into God's purposes for creating us. In these chapters we find God blessing Adam and Eve, talking with them, sharing His love with them. It is a hauntingly beautiful scene of a tender Creator placing man and woman in a garden.

There is humor, too, in the Creation story. After God had finished everything, the record states that He gathered the animals and birds—which must have been an amazing feat, as well as an interesting sight—and "he brought them to the man to see what he would name them; and whatever the man called each living creature, that was its name" (Gen. 2:19, N.I.V.). Is it making God too much like us to picture Him having a marvelous time, laughing with Adam as the animals paraded by and Adam pioneered in giving each its original name? God must have rejoiced to watch Adam use his brand-new brain to form names for the animals and birds. But this delightful episode would have been impossible if man had had no power of choice!

It was impossible for Adam and Eve, even with perfect natures, to have their love and loyalty tested and developed unless there was opportunity for them to make a choice between right and wrong. If they, with undeveloped but perfect characters, were placed in this sin-free environment with no opportunity to make a wrong choice, they really could never mature or develop properly. Physical muscles need to be challenged in order to develop strength. So with their moral "muscles."

God provided that opportunity by placing in the

Garden a tree, which the Bible calls a "tree of knowledge of good and evil." Adam and Eve were permitted to eat freely of the fruit of all the other trees, save this one, lone tree. They were clearly warned that the penalty for disobeying God is death. A severe penalty, but it couldn't have been any other way. Disobedience of any rule God sets forth eventually leads to death, whether it be physical laws, health laws, or moral laws. God created man to operate properly only if certain rules were followed. Every purchaser of a new car receives an owner's manual that gives detailed instructions for its care and maintenance. Obedience to these instructions is the only way for the owner to have satisfactory performance. Disregard inevitably spells trouble. So it is with man. God, who created man, also wrote out the instructions, which if obeyed would yield joy, happiness, and eternal life. Disobedience would result in sin, sickness, disease, and death.

The same inspired record that tells of man's perfect creation also tells how he disobeyed God and ate the forbidden fruit. The result is all too evident. This was the great tragedy of the ages, that man would take the freedom given him for his good and use it to disobey his Creator. Mind you, nothing was wrong with the fruit—the only thing wrong was the act of disobedience, self-will, rebellion. In fact, when Adam and Eve ate the forbidden fruit, they were really saying to God that He was wrong and they were right! They were telling God, "You are a liar!" They were telling God, "We are gods, too; we have a life of our own. We know what's best for ourselves. We can live, move, and breathe apart from You. We don't need You!" The basic ingredient of all sin is independence from God. The result? The only thing that could happen—death.

Death, you see, is not simply an arbitrary penalty for sin. God didn't capriciously decide on this awful penalty as the proper one for disobedience. God is the Source of life. From the minutest to the most complex forms, life owes not only its existence but its maintenance and its support to God. No grain of wheat has a life of its own. No dog, flower, insect, or person has a life of its own. All life is borrowed from God, the Source of life. The moment one separates himself from that life, to be independent of it, death is the only possible consequence. No light bulb can be unscrewed from its socket and continue to burn!

When he sinned, man cut off the limb on which he was sitting. He fell and became incapable and unwilling to do right. No doubt the transformation was not instantaneous, but his perfect nature now became imperfect. His spiritual nature was perverted. Selfishness instead of love now ruled. He became a captive to Satan.

And when Adam fell, every one of his descendants, including you and me, fell with him. We fell into darkness, sin, and death. Some feel this is unjust. Why should everybody suffer because of one man? The facts are that Adam and Eve could not bequeath to their children something they didn't have themselves. Life produces its own kind. Spiders don't produce butterflies, nor do sinful parents produce sinless children. Sin is a self-multiplying force. Furthermore, since that awful day, each person has proved this point

29

by sinning. Paul expresses it this way: "Sin entered the world through one man, and death through sin, and in this way death came to all men, because all sinned" (Rom. 5:12, N.I.V.). John agrees with Paul: "If we claim to be without sin, we deceive ourselves and the truth is not in us" (1 John 1:8, N.I.V.).

Man, whom God designed for such a marvelous potential, has become man the failure, the sinner. The next chapter will discuss God's plan for saving mankind as announced in the three angels' messages of Revelation 14.

---

* Page 17ff. (New York: Macmillan, 1952).

Fig Leaves
and the
Everlasting Gospel

Everyone seems to recognize that something is wrong with mankind. But few seem to understand the causes as set forth in the previous chapter or the steps that God plans to take to restore men and women to their original sinless state. God put this plan into operation as soon as sin began, and thus it is called in Scripture "the everlasting gospel." This gospel is found in a special setting in the first angel's message.

Notice how John introduces this angel and its message: "And I saw another angel fly in the midst of heaven, having the everlasting gospel to preach unto them that dwell on the earth, and to every nation, and kindred, and tongue, and people, saying with a loud voice, Fear God, and give glory to him; for the hour of his judgment is come: and worship him that made heaven, and earth, and the sea, and the fountains of waters" (Rev. 14:6, 7).

It is interesting that the "everlasting gospel" appears as the keynote or theme of these messages. Actually, as we unfold the symbolism of these three messages, we will find that the gospel is crucial to understanding the issues. John calls it the "everlasting" gospel. It is the same gospel that has thrilled the hearts of sinners ever since Adam and Eve disobeyed their Creator; the same gospel that was delivered to Enoch, Noah, Abraham, Daniel, and the New Testament apostles; the same gospel that has been handed down to us today. The gospel at the end of time is identical to the gospel at the very beginning. God's purposes for man have never changed. Neither has His gospel. His plan for saving us from sin and death has consistently remained the same in spite of all the attempts by Satan to thwart it and in spite of man's stubbornness and blindness.

The solemn announcements and warnings found in the second and third angels' messages (as we will examine later) must be seen in the context of right versus wrong; the true, everlasting gospel as opposed to a false gospel (or gospels). In vivid contrast to the principles of the "everlasting gospel" is a religious system led by an apostate Christianity that fabricates "every wind of doctrine" (Eph. 4:14). Revelation 14:12 draws this distinction with almost painful clarity. After describing the awful punishments reserved for those who accept the beast and its mark, John says, "Here is the patience of the saints: here are they that keep the commandments of God, and the faith of Jesus."

Whatever precise identification one gives to the "beast" and his "mark," it must be ever kept in mind that the basic concept is the irreconcilable conflict between the truth of the "everlasting gospel" on the one hand and the deceptive cunning of the beast and its counterfeit gospel on the other. This same conflict has been seen ever since sin began on earth.

When Adam and Eve distrusted and disobeyed their Creator and allowed sin to come into their lives and into the perfect earth, their first reaction was to try to hide from God. Sin causes fear and shame. The covering of light and purity that had previously been theirs disappeared, and they realized their naked condition. Genesis 3:7 says that they made crude coverings of leaves to hide their nakedness. The natural tendency of the sinful human heart ever since has been to try to make up our own deficiencies, to justify ourselves, to earn approval by our own actions. The innocence Adam and Eve had lost through sin they tried to recapture by their own efforts. This same principle has been the basis for every false gospel. Whether it is the heathen offering food to an idol, a hermit secluding himself from society and denying the needs of the body, or a twentieth-century secularist who feels that he alone is responsible for himself and that there is no God—the natural impulse of man is to seek salvation on his own terms and by his own efforts. This is the principle at the heart of the system ruled over by the beast. The "everlasting gospel"— God's method of salvation for man—is entirely different.

After Adam and Eve had fashioned makeshift coverings for themselves in a vain effort to undo the effects of their sin, God came looking for them. He still loved them in spite of their sin against Him. In love He caused them to see their sin and admit their helplessness. Then He prepared garments of animal skins for them to cover the nakedness sin had caused (see Gen. 3:21).

The lesson is clear. Man cannot atone for his own sins; only God can provide a covering. The salvation that He gives is entirely without human devising; man can only act. But notice that it is a costly arrangement. It requires a death. "The wages of sin is death" (Rom. 6:23). An animal had to die in order to provide coverings for that first guilty pair. This symbolized the death of God's own Son, Jesus Christ, who would give His life for sinners.

In a most dramatic way God impressed this truth upon the minds of the first couple. Adam was ordered to slay an animal with his own hands. He had never seen a dead flower before, let alone a dead animal. He had never contemplated death or the horrible idea that he would be required to take life. Imagine his remorse as he took the life of an innocent animal. The act of killing must have left Adam shaken as he realized that *his* sin had caused the death of this animal.

From the skin of the slain sacrifice God made clothing for Adam and Eve. This gift of clothing made by God replaced the makeshift leaf garments fashioned by man. As we envision Adam and Eve wearing these clothes, we can be conscious of two things: payment for sin requires the death of Jesus, symbolized by an animal sacrifice; and righteousness and eternal life are possible only as a gift, symbolized by the clothing made and given to them by God.

Throughout the Bible clothing is repeatedly used as a symbol of the righteousness of Jesus. Isaiah said, "He hath clothed me with the garments of salvation, he hath covered me with the robe of righteousness" (Isa. 61:10).

Thus from the very beginning God did everything possible to clearly show that man is totally powerless to save himself. Man is powerless to change his own life, powerless to cover his sins, powerless to justify himself, powerless to make himself righteous! Salvation is God taking action in behalf of man. Adam and Eve did not make their robes; they only killed the animal. What a fearful price they paid for operating on the mark-of-the-beast principle!

This same contrast between the "everlasting gospel" and Satan's counterfeit can be seen in Adam and Eve's children. God made clear to them that a Saviour would come to deliver them from their sins by dying in their place. They were to exhibit their acceptance and faith in this salvation by offering a lamb as a sacrifice. Just as the innocent lamb would die, so the Lamb of God would die as their unblemished substitute.

The early record of the Scripture describes how in the course of time Cain and Abel, sons of Adam and Eve, brought a sacrifice to God. Abel obediently killed a lamb as his offering. Cain, on the other hand, did not think it important to follow God's specific command and brought instead an offering of the fruits and vegetables he had grown. When God failed to accept his offering, he became angry, even though he, not God, was at fault. He became so angry, in fact, that he killed his righteous brother Abel, who attempted to persuade him to obey God.

Here is the outworking of the same principle that motivates the beast and its followers. Instead of accepting by faith God's plan of salvation, they attempt

35

to deal with sin and to find salvation by their own efforts. There is no faith in a Substitute; they seek to gain salvation by their own works. Opposition to their false gospel provokes the same reaction that occurred in Cain—anger, and a willingness to persecute and silence those who are faithful to God.

In His infinite wisdom God devised a means of dealing with the problem of sin that would not only demonstrate His justice and vindicate His character but would result in the complete restoration of every sinner who accepts the provisions of His salvation. That plan has at its very center the voluntary sacrifice of His own Son, Jesus Christ, who freely gave Himself in man's place. The Incarnation, the cross, the resurrection, the Second Coming, are the grand, focal points of Scripture; they beautifully declare that nothing is of greater importance than the redemption of mankind. This is the theme, the gospel, of Scripture. Although proclaimed in a thousand ways through prophecy and parable, the point is that nothing can excel, or even equal, the "everlasting gospel." For that reason nothing could be more execrable than a perversion of that gospel. What could equal in danger and deceptive terribleness a false plan of salvation that results not in salvation but in damnation? Jesus asked, "'What good is it for a man to gain the whole world, yet forfeit his soul?'" (Mark 8:36, N.I.V.). Jesus came, lived, died, and was resurrected for the express purpose of seeking and saving "that which was lost" (Luke 19:10).

When we contemplate the mystery of redemption—the unbelievable love of God for a rebellious world—we must kneel before the Father and pray with Paul for power to "grasp how wide and long and high and deep is the love of Christ, and to know this love that surpasses knowledge" (Eph. 3:18, 19, N.I.V.). "God was in Christ, reconciling the world unto himself" (2 Cor. 5:19). From beginning to end the "everlasting gospel" is the core, the theme, the foundation, of Scripture. It is the focal point of heaven, and it should receive the constant attention of all mankind. Our business and joy is to know the true gospel as a living experience in our own lives and to communicate this glorious truth in a loving and persuasive manner to others.

The controversy that has raged since the very beginning of sin and that comes to a climax in these angels' messages centers upon the understanding or misunderstanding of the "everlasting gospel." This is the reason for the first angel's proclamation of the gospel to every person on earth. Thus is also emphasized the importance of having a clear understanding of the gospel.

Later in this book we will be looking in detail at God's plan of salvation, the gospel that has come down to us from the very beginning. Reduced to its most simple expression it is "believe on the Lord Jesus Christ, and thou shalt be saved" (Acts 16:31), "for there is none other name under heaven given among men, whereby we must be saved" (chap. 4:12). This salvation does not come as a result of our actions. We cannot earn it by our works or deserve it; it comes as the free gift of God's grace. "Not by works of righteousness which we have done, but according to his mercy he saved us" (Titus 3:5). "For by grace are ye saved through faith; and that not of yourselves: it is the gift of God: not of works, lest any man should boast" (Eph. 2:8, 9).

The first angel, then, appeals to every man, woman, and child to accept the "everlasting gospel," to accept God's gracious offer of salvation and refuse the mark of the beast, which is salvation by works of self-righteousness.

But that isn't all that the angel said. John heard the angel exclaim, " 'Fear God and give him glory . . . ; and worship him who made heaven and earth, the sea and the fountains of water' " (Rev. 14:7, R.S.V.).

What does it mean to "fear" God? Should we be afraid of someone as loving and merciful as our heavenly Father? Should we cringe like a puppy expecting a kick? What has God done to us that we should be afraid of Him? He loves us! He sent Jesus to die for us!

The verb "to fear" can also mean "to reverence" or "to hold in awe." What the angel means here is that we should feel the solemn majesty of the divine Creator and reverence Him. If you should receive a formal invitation to meet the Queen of England or the President of the United States, wouldn't you be a little nervous just before you actually came into the presence of such an important person? You would know you really had nothing to fear, yet you would be somewhat frightened at such a meeting, wouldn't you? Of course! And how much more important God is than all the presidents and queens and kings of earth combined!

We live every moment of our lives under the watchfulness of God; He knows everything about us. How much we ought to reverence Him and stand in awe of His incomprehensible majesty, His divine power, His matchless love and grace!

We need to give glory to Him, not only with our voices but in our actions as well. By gladly obeying Him and allowing Him to reproduce His character in our lives, we glorify the One who gave us life and who has saved us from eternal death.

We have said that the "everlasting gospel" reduced to its simplest terms is salvation by faith in Jesus Christ apart from any works of righteousness on our part. The mark-of-the-beast principle is the counterfeit, or salvation by human effort. A counterfeit, however, must closely resemble the genuine. No one would be foolish enough to make counterfeit $18 notes. Why not? Because there is no genuine $18 note! A counterfeit depends for its very existence on a close likeness to the genuine. So it is with Satan's counterfeit plan of salvation. He knows that how a person lives *is* important. He knows that the person who has accepted the free grace of God by faith for salvation will not then continue to live without regard to obeying God's commandments. So he very subtly makes a seemingly minor change in the genuine gospel and produces a counterfeit. From a gospel in which good works have their place as the *fruit* of salvation, Satan and his agent, the beast, develop a gospel in which works are the *source* of salvation. It seems to be only a slight alteration, but it makes a profound difference. In the genuine, salvation comes as God's free gift without regard to the works that we do, and then obedience follows as an expression of gratitude and as a natural outgrowth of salvation. In the counterfeit, salvation depends on the works that one does.

It is because obedience *is* important to God that Satan has twisted it to serve his own perverted gospel.

The three angels' messages, then, put obedience in its rightful place as an important element in the life of those who have experienced God's salvation. "Worship him who made heaven and earth, the sea and the fountains of water" (Rev. 14:7, R.S.V.). God is calling on every person on earth to reverence Him and glorify Him by faithful obedience to His commandments, rather than giving themselves to serve the beast. It is a call to decision!

The Lord bases His claim to our allegiance and worship and obedience on the fact that He is our Creator. He gave us life, and therefore we owe everything to Him. Over and over again, God dismisses the pagan gods as unworthy of worship because they have no power to give life or to care for their followers. Only the self-existent, eternal Creator deserves our worship.

"For thus says the Lord, who created the heavens (he is God!), who formed the earth and made it (he established it; he did not create it a chaos, he formed it to be inhabited!): 'I am the Lord, and there is no other. . . . They have no knowledge who carry about their wooden idols, and keep on praying to a god that cannot save. . . . Turn to me and be saved, all the ends of the earth! For I am God, and there is no other'" (Isa.

40

45:18-22, R.S.V.).

God deserves our worship because we owe our existence to Him. We have no life except by His constant, creative power. This is why the angel who gives this first message points to God as the Creator when pleading with the people of earth to worship Him.

How do we worship God? If we go to church once a week and pray three times a day, have we worshiped Him? If we speak of our love for Him, have we worshiped?

In marriage the bride and groom promise to love, cherish, and honor each other. How do they do so in actual practice? Is carrying out the garbage fulfilling the marriage vow? Has a wife kept her promise when she has cooked three meals a day for six weeks? Has her husband cherished her by faithfully bringing home his paycheck and supporting her? Marriage certainly includes all of these things, but it is more than any one of them—much more. Marriage is a total giving of one's self to the marriage partner and doing so happily, not grudgingly.

Likewise, worshiping God involves much more than a mechanical obedience. Worship is a total giving of one's self to God. It is a way of life, a fundamental loyalty. Worship is complete obedience in heart and mind to our Creator, and doing so happily. Jesus said, "'If you love me, you will keep my commandments'" (John 14:15, R.S.V.). The apostle John wrote in another place, "For this is the love of God, that we keep his commandments. And his commandments are not burdensome" (1 John 5:3, R.S.V.). We cannot worship God while willfully disobeying Him.

The issue is clear: The first angel appeals to men to worship the Creator and receive His seal. The third angel (as we will see) gives a dire warning against receiving the mark of the beast power opposed to God and His gospel.

The first angel's message, if accepted seriously into the heart and life, will do for us what it has done for many others through the long centuries. We are called to worship the Creator, the glorious One, the only One who can give us life and keep us alive, the only One who can change our hearts and keep them changed. This message is a mighty promise of God's power, to be made available to all who claim it by faith.

Here God shows His great love for His created beings. He wants everyone to be saved who will come to Him. That's why He sends messages of such urgency that they are represented as being carried by angels flying through the sky. He wants everyone to be aware of the issues involved, so He gives a final plea for men and women to accept Jesus Christ and His righteousness. Even the messages of the second and third angels, bringing as they do solemn and straightforward denunciations and warnings, exhibit God's undying love. This we will see in later chapters.

Is
Change
Possible?

Have you ever considered all the things and occupations that exist in our lives because of the introduction of sin into our planet? The list is seemingly endless—keys, locks, banks, jails, hospitals, guards, insurance policies, cemeteries, undertakers, lawyers, pesticides, doctors, nurses, druggists, exterminators, preachers, fire engines, window screens, guns, ambulances, armies, navies, air forces, even clothes and cosmetics! And these are just a few! It seems we spend most of our energies and time on events and occupations that are related to the sin problem. But the worst effect sin has caused is the changing of man's nature, and here is the crux of all earth's problems.

Most sociologists and psychologists emphasize the importance of environment. If you put a person into the right environment, they insist, most of his problems will be solved. Is this true? If poverty causes crime (and certainly it *can* aggravate it), then why is there an enormous rise in crime statistics among middle- and upper-class youth who have plenty of money, fancy homes, and late-model cars? If every gun or other weapon on earth were destroyed, would this bring a halt to murder and war? It might improve the statistics somewhat, but as long as folks have two hands (or even one hand) and can find a club, a stone, or something similar, they will continue to destroy life! The apostle James makes an interesting comment on this point. "What causes fights and quarrels among you? Don't they come from your desires that battle within you?" (James 4:1, N.I.V.).

If God packed up the entire human race and transported it to the perfect environment of heaven, would this solve the sin problem? All God would accomplish by this act would be the contamination of heaven. We must understand that there is a hereditary factor to the sin problem. In man's nature there is bias toward evil, a force that he cannot resist without outside aid.

So what is the answer? How *does* God deal with the sin problem? Do you remember the idea that Jesus expressed about making a tree good and then its fruit will be good? Ah, there is the answer! Change the man, and his actions will change! But someone exclaims, "Is it not incredible to think that a person can change so drastically? The evidence is not overwhelming that such a change of nature can take place. One can find liars, thieves, adulterers, child abusers, drunkards, practicing homosexuals, and gamblers even among professed Christians."

It's true that the lives of Christians do not always give evidence of a change. We have only to look into our own lives as Christians to know how far short we come of God's ideal. Even Christ's disciples were skeptical of the idea that man could be changed. Jesus had just told a rich young man that he had a problem. No, he didn't murder, commit adultery, steal, or lie; but his nature was greedy. He was rich, and his greedy, sinful nature rebelled against the idea of sharing his wealth with the poor. Notice that from all outward appearance this man was a model person. He scrupulously kept all the commandments. There probably isn't a Christian church in the world today that would refuse him baptism and membership just as he was, without any change in his nature. His outward actions were good. But greediness and covetousness is a problem that isn't as visible as is murder or stealing.

Yet this poor rich fellow had a nature that needed to be changed before he could qualify for God's kingdom. In fact, his problem was so severe that the Lord said to His disciples, " 'It is easier for a camel to go through the eye of a needle than for a rich man to enter the kingdom of God.' "

How did the disciples respond? "They were greatly astonished and asked, 'Who then can be saved?' " In other words, "Is it possible for a man's nature to be changed?"

The answer Jesus gave was positive and wonderfully encouraging. He said, " 'With man this is impossible, but with God all things are possible' " (Matt. 19:24-26, N.I.V.).

" 'With God all things are possible.' " This is the key to salvation! That short, pithy statement contains several important basic truths. First, it tells us that salvation centers not on man but on God. When we speak of the seal of God, it is *God's* seal, *God's* work,

45

not man's. But in contrast, when the mark of the beast comes into view, God is not in the picture at all. It is the beast power, not God, that marks its followers. In other words, the way of true salvation is God-centered, while the mark principle is man-centered. (Remember the beast symbolism is that of a man-made system.)

We can say this another way. The true way of salvation is by grace through faith in Christ. It is the Lord's work; He is the One who does the saving. In the mark-of-the-beast system, salvation revolves around man and what he can do to save himself. It is salvation by works, a man-centered system.

Now we have established two principles on which to build. One is that man's nature is degraded and needs to be changed. The second is that change is possible, as Jesus flatly stated, " 'With God all things are possible.' "

In the great "change" chapter of Scripture—John 3—Jesus was conversing at night with a most prominent teacher and church leader, Nicodemus. This man's outward conformity to the law was in all probability nearly perfect. The Scriptures do not say so, but as a member of the Jewish ruling council, Nicodemus was undoubtedly a good husband, father, citizen, and neighbor. It isn't hard to imagine him as honest, generous, kind, and helpful. He was greatly respected. He was a model man! Every preacher I know would have been excited had Nicodemus come to his church and applied for membership. What an honor to have a man of this caliber in the church, one whose outward actions were so circumspect! Think of the moral and financial support he would give!

But Jesus read his heart and saw a far different picture. Nicodemus was ostensibly looking for instruction, but he needed salvation. Jesus made it clear that only regeneration—a change of his mind and heart, not mere information—would solve his problem. If you read the whole story, you will note that Jesus sounded at times like a broken record, for He repeated the new-birth concept at least five times. Jesus told Nicodemus plainly that if he wanted to see the kingdom of God, he "must be born again" (verse 7). That is how important the new birth is. The word *must* is nonnegotiable; there is no way around it. The new birth and eternal life are inseparable. This is not a popular truth, but it is the basis of the unalterable prerequisite for entrance into the kingdom of God. It makes absolutely no difference how great your ancestry is, how high on the social ladder you may stand, how much you are worth in cash and investments, what kind of car you drive, or what contacts you have with influential people in the military, industry, or government; unless you are "born again" you cannot enter God's kingdom.

The words *born again* have been overworked in our society. There are some who go around continually talking about being born-again Christians. They infuriate people by asking, "Have you been born again?" It is easy to talk of the new birth, but what does it mean to be born again? More important, how does one arrive at this born-again experience?

The term is a figure of speech Jesus used with Nicodemus, but it has other equivalents. Conversion and regeneration are two. Peter, preaching to the crowd that gathered after his healing a lame man at the Temple gate, said, "Repent . . . , and be coverted" (Acts 3:19). The word *convert* means simply "to turn about" or "to change direction." This involves a turning to God in conduct as well as in mind. Thus a change in nature is implied. Paul uses several terms to describe the new-birth experience. One is "regeneration" and the other is "new creation" (see Titus 3:5; 2 Cor. 5:17, R.S.V.). Regardless of what term is used—"new birth," "conversion," "regeneration," or "new creation"—the concept includes a change of nature.

Just as one has no control over his natural birth or any part in it, so the new birth is a supernatural work of God on the sinful human heart. In fact, it is a mysterious action. In His conversation with Nicodemus Jesus compared the work of the Holy Spirit on the human heart to the wind blowing. We can hear the wind; we can see the effects of the wind; but we do not understand where it comes from or where it goes. "So is every one that is born of the Spirit" (John 3:8).

Notice again that this changing of man's nature is *God's* work, not man's! Remember, "With God all things are possible." We can't change our hearts. We can't change the deepest motives of our minds. But God can!

God is the initiator of the whole salvation process. When Adam and Eve sinned, their first impulse was to hide. They hid their nakedness with a flimsy covering of leaves, then they tried to hide from God in the recesses of the Garden! Man has been hiding and running from God ever since then. Man is alienated from God and at enmity with Him because of sin. As sinners, Paul says, we have been "alienated from the life of God" (Eph. 4:18). Again he states, "All of us . . . were by nature objects of wrath" (chap. 2:3, N.I.V.). Again, "The sinful mind is hostile to God. It does not submit to God's law, nor can it do so. Those controlled by the sinful nature cannot please God" (Rom. 8:7, 8, N.I.V.). Thus the Bible gives strong evidence that any change for the better in our relationship with God starts with *God*, not us! God has taken the initiative and has invaded enemy territory at the expense of the death of His own Son, Jesus Christ, in order to win alienated man back to Himself.

We should ever keep in mind that God went in search of man, not man in search of God. One of the most touching parables Jesus ever told was the story of the shepherd who had a hundred sheep. When one was lost, Jesus asked His listeners, " 'Does he not leave the ninety-nine in the open country and go after the lost sheep until he finds it?' " (See Luke 15:3-7, N.I.V.)

Jesus is the Shepherd—we are the lost sheep. In fact, our whole world is a lost sheep, and "God so loved the world, that he gave his only begotten Son" (John 3:16) for it. In His great love God has made the first move. "God commendeth his love toward us, in that, while we were yet sinners, Christ died for us" (Rom. 5:8).

Too many discouraged people, lost sheep, feel they must repent or be good *before* God's love is extended to them. No! No! Jesus tried to dispel this terrible concept, and in so doing was criticized by the religious leaders who said, with biting disdain, "'This man welcomes sinners and eats with them'" (Luke 15:2, N.I.V.).

This is why this point is so important. If a person has the idea he must change *before* he comes to God, he will never come, or he will come on his own terms—works! He will attempt to make himself worthy to come to God. That's what we call salvation by works, and it is at the heart of the system symbolized by the beast. To think that we *earn* the right to come to God, that we *deserve* to be in the kingdom, is the position taken by those who receive the mark of the beast. But the moment they do, they obviate the plan of salvation.

The truth of the matter is, that "there is no one who understands, no one who seeks God. All have turned away" (Rom. 3:11, 12, N.I.V.). But when we see the Saviour as a loving Shepherd searching for us, it produces, if we will let it, a response of love in our hearts for Him. Anyone who has permitted himself to be found by the Lord knows the truth of Paul's words: "Do you show contempt for the riches of his kindness, tolerance and patience, not realizing that God's kindness leads toward repentance?" (chap. 2:4, N.I.V.).

This principle of God as the One initiating the action to save us cannot be emphasized too strongly. If this point is missed, the plan of salvation won't make sense. A change in our lives is impossible until we capture this concept and understand it thoroughly. No matter how wicked or awful a person has been, the Saviour is seeking for him. And when he is found, bruised, bleeding, and wounded, the Good Shepherd tenderly takes him in His arms and with great joy carries him back to the fold of safety. O what a magnificent Saviour we have! With our human limitations it is impossible to understand such love.

The
Brass
Serpent

Have you ever had friends over to visit and found the conversation turning to how the wives and husbands first met, fell in love, and finally married? If you are happily married, you have probably told many times your experience of meeting, dating, and marrying your spouse. But have you ever performed a thorough, objective analysis on your love experience, in which you listed all the steps in precise order—put each ingredient into the test tube, so to speak—and ended up with a neat little recipe that would be applicable to all love stories that ended in marriage?

Ridiculous, you say! And you are right. In fact, you cannot even properly evaluate and categorize all the steps in your own experience, much less come up with a scientific equation for love and marriage that is guaranteed to work for others. No, the love story of any couple is unique to them. Oh, of course there are certain things about love that have a common denominator. I think all ladies appreciate gifts of flowers, unless they are allergic to them! But in general there is a unique pattern for each couple.

The same is true of salvation. There are all kinds of theories about how God saves a person. I've heard some well-meaning ministers try to explain the precise steps in salvation as if they were explaining the scientific basis for constructing an atomic bomb. They have all the details worked out in orderly fashion, and if you follow their equation to the letter, the promise of heaven is yours. Now, that sounds nice, but actually the story of salvation is as unique to an individual as is his love experience with his spouse. People fell in love, got married, and had happy homes long before marriage counselors and psychologists came along to tell them what to do (or why they did what they did) in order to have a happy marriage. I believe that even if every book on marriage disappeared tomorrow, men and women would still meet each other, fall in love, get married, have children, and live happily ever after.

So it is in the realm of salvation. Long before theologians analyzed and gave exact descriptions to Biblical terminology, people were meeting God and experiencing a genuine love relationship with Him, although they didn't understand or even know all the exact steps to salvation.

Now, having said that, I'm going to try to do what I just said can't really be done! I'm going to list various steps and elements in the salvation process according to the Scriptures. Now, mind you, what I shall share comes from Scripture and my own experience. Each experience is slightly different, but I shall lay down broad guidelines and trust that God's Spirit will speak to your heart as He has to mine.

Salvation is a personal experience. It is as ridiculous to argue about it as it would be for a young man to argue with his fiancée over points of falling in love! Yet I have heard mature, intelligent, educated people argue over the exact process of salvation as if it were a combination lock and all one had to do was to find the exact combination and heaven would open. God just doesn't work that way.

In the story of Nicodemus, this teacher asked, "'How can a man be born when he is old?'" Jesus said, "'You should not be surprised at my saying, "You must be born again"'" (see John 3:1-17, N.I.V.). Then Jesus used the illustration of the wind, which He compared to the operation of the Holy Spirit on the human heart. Now nothing is really too logical about wind. Most of us never think of analyzing the wind by using certain formulas to show in detail exactly how the wind operates and in which direction it's going to blow. About all we know of the wind is that it exists and that we can witness its effects on nature. What I am trying to say is that no two conversion experiences are identical any more than two fingerprints are identical.

There *are* broad general principles that are ingredients in all conversion experiences, but there is one grand element at the center, the focal point, of salvation—Jesus Christ. This element exists in all conversion experiences. When we get so wrapped up in dissecting the various steps of salvation or when we become lopsided and emphasize one step almost to the exclusion of others, and in the process forget the One who made it all possible, we miss salvation. *Christ*— not repentance, confession, justification, or sanctification—is our salvation. We don't praise the gospels; we praise Jesus. We don't worship any or all of the steps of salvation, but we worship the Lord of salvation. Some make the mistake of letting the cross of Christ obscure the Christ of the cross.

Back to our love story again. Two lovers never speak of their love experience in terms of some particular action or thing. Never. A *person* is always at the core of a love experience. The central theme of a husband's love is his *wife*, not her perfume or hair or the way she says goodnight. Of course, these things (as well as many others) are important, but they are not the *heart* of the love experience. The person is!

So when we speak of certain elements of salvation, remember they all center in the person of Jesus Christ. I've tried to emphasize this by pointing out that Jesus, the Father, and the Holy Spirit agreed together to save man. They made the first step to find their lost sheep. Jesus committed Himself to be the Saviour of man "from the foundation of the world" (Rev. 13:8). The Father chose Jesus as the Saviour "before the foundation of the world" (1 Peter 1:20).

Furthermore, God planned to save all men, not just a few. God wants "all men to be saved, and to come unto the knowledge of the truth" (1 Tim. 2:4). Jesus died for the sins of the whole world. All of us are sinners, "for all have sinned, and come short of the glory of God" (Rom. 3:23). The glorious truth is that it is absolutely impossible for any sinner to be lost if he does not resist the magnetic drawing power of Jesus. We are all predestined, if you please, to be saved. There is no favoritism with God.

But you ask, "Will everybody be saved?"

I wish I could answer "Yes!" But the human heart

is stubborn. Paul, speaking to his own people, who had a knowledge of God, said, "But because of your stubbornness and your unrepentant heart, you are storing up wrath against yourself for the day of God's wrath, when his righteous judgment will be revealed" (chap. 2:5, N.I.V.). In this text you will notice the word *unrepentant*. That word gives us an important clue to one of the events that take place in the life of one who is saved. The opposite of "unrepentant" is "repentant." What does the word mean? It means turning around—changing your mind and your life. What do we mean by a change of mind? It means that our mind's attitude becomes one of tenderness and love toward God.

This is not at all a mere sentimental attitude composed of nothing more than pure emotion. I once had a barber who was a rough type of fellow but who professed to be a Christian. The gulf between the way he lived and his profession of Christ was wider than the Grand Canyon. But the strange thing about him was that every time I mentioned the name *Jesus* in his presence, tears would immediately come to his eyes. It seemed to be a sort of Pavlovian reflex action he had developed over the years. I cannot judge his heart, of course, but his words and actions certainly needed changing if they were to be in harmony with the life of a follower of Jesus. Repentance means more than tears in the eyes; it means a change in the life.

Repentance, then, inevitably includes a turning away from sin, not because you feel you must, but because you want to. There is a change in your mind toward evil. The other day I saw a mother cuddling her tiny, nearly new baby. The way her face broadcast love for that infant was touching and inspiring. Suppose I had asked, "Do you have to force yourself to act that way toward your child?" She would have been insulted, and rightly so. So it is with repentance—the heart or mind is flooded with love toward God.

The question is, How can a sinner repent? What causes him to change his mind? It is as impossible for a person to bring about this change for himself as it is for a black man to make himself white or vice versa. That's exactly what the Bible says. "Can the Ethiopian change his skin, or the leopard its spots? Neither can you do good who are accustomed to doing evil" (Jer. 13:23, N.I.V.).

Therefore something must precede repentance. Actually, God, through the Holy Spirit, gives repentance to us as a free gift. But He can do so only if we, in faith, look to Jesus and accept the repentance God offers. And it is probably at this point, more than any other, where the most failures occur in becoming and remaining a Christian. It is difficult for the human heart to accept its helplessness and depend solely on Someone else. Actually, it is right at this point that I am the weakest and most vulnerable, and I think the same is true for most Christians.

This point is made in a variety of ways throughout the Scriptures. We will start with the way Jesus underscored this point to Nicodemus in John 3:14, 15: "And as Moses lifted up the serpent in the wilderness, even so must the Son of man be lifted up: that whosoever believeth in him should not perish, but have eternal life."

MARKED!

What is the background for this unusual text? When Israel was miraculously delivered from Egypt, the people were led through the Sinai Desert. The whole journey was a series of miracles: God fed them angels' food, bread from heaven; provided pure water from flinty rock; placed over them a cloud cover for shade by day and a warm cover of fire by night in this inhospitable desert. In spite of these extraordinary life-sustaining benefits, what do you think the people did? They miserably complained not only against Moses but against God Himself. So the Lord withdrew His protection, and poisonous snakes began to crawl into their camp and bite the people. Many died.

The terrified Israelites were repentant and changed their minds about God and Moses. They cried, "We have sinned, for we have spoken against the Lord, and against thee; pray unto the Lord, that he take away the serpents from us. And Moses prayed for the people." (See Num. 21:4-9.)

The Lord instructed Moses to erect a pole with a brass serpent on top. Then He required the people to look upon this brass serpent if they wanted deliverance. What a scene—yet it is a scene that is being repeated today. The plan of salvation is contained in this story. Look in simple faith to Jesus for the healing so desperately needed.

Some looked, and some didn't. Those who by faith took God at His word and looked at the serpent were healed. Those who had no faith in being healed by simply looking, died.

Can you see the picture? Fathers and mothers, brothers and sisters, were scurrying about, encouraging their neighbors or relatives to believe and look. How awful it must have been to hear some say, "It's no use. I'm dying, and looking at a piece of brass on a pole is absolutely absurd. It will never help me. Let me alone so I may die in peace!" What a fatal decision!

The lesson is clear. There was no healing virtue in the brass object itself. It was the person's faith in God that made the difference. Believing in God's word, obeying His command, and looking in faith emancipated the sick person from death!

When Jesus used this illustration, He was sharing with Nicodemus both the source and the results of the new-birth experience. Nicodemus, being a highly educated Jewish teacher, was familiar with the snake story. The lessons in the story were obvious to him and even to us, so I will enumerate only a few of them:

1. The wound of sin cannot be healed by any works the sinner tries to perform.

2. There is no scientific basis for healing by looking.

3. Even though we may not be able to arrange the steps for salvation chronologically, doubtless the first giant step is to look by faith to Jesus.

4. All other attempts to be saved, other than by lifting up Christ in the wilderness of our own hearts and looking in faith to Him, are fatal and part of the mark-of-the-beast system.

5. Like Nicodemus, who learned the lesson well, we must search the Scriptures in a way that leads us to *Christ* as the center of salvation.

6. Controversy regarding the logic or necessity of God's plan of salvation leads to death, not life. Rather,

there is life in a look to Him.

7. Look not to self, with all of its defects and wounds, but rely on the merits of Christ alone, and the help we need will be ours. If we look at the snakebites of sin, we will only get worse and die.

8. Do not wait until every detail of salvation is plain before looking to Jesus. Don't continue wandering in philosophical doubts and fears. Rather, look *now* in simple faith to the Saviour, who became "sin for us" (2 Cor. 5:21). (That's the reason why the brass serpent was made in the image of a snake, not the image of a person.)

It sounds incredibly wonderful, doesn't it? But wait a moment! The greatest battle facing every sinner is overlooking or not looking to Jesus. Paul employs a battle term to illustrate this point. "Fight the good fight of faith, lay hold on eternal life" (1 Tim. 6:12). The "fight of faith" is the struggle to look to Jesus rather than focusing on our temptations. It is a battle to look to Jesus by faith alone. Oh, it is so much easier to look at our trials, our problems, our weaknesses, husband, wife, children, money, TV, sex—the list is endless! It is so much easier to *do* something rather than to *look* at something to be saved. It is so much easier to doubt than to believe. It is so much easier to study the Bible for information rather than for inspiration and salvation. So the poor human race struggles on in doubts, fears, and perplexities, waiting to die from its wounds rather than "fight the good fight of faith." Look to Jesus.

The famous preacher Charles Spurgeon relates his experience of conversion: "The minister did not come that morning; he was snowed up, I suppose. At last, a very thin-looking man, a shoemaker, or tailor, or something of that sort, went up into the pulpit to preach. Now, it is well that preachers should be instructed; but this man was really stupid. He was obliged to stick to his text, for the simple reason that he had little else to say. The text was, 'Look unto me, and be ye saved, all the ends of the earth' (Isa. 45:22). He did not even pronounce the words rightly, but that did not matter. There was, I thought, a glimpse of hope for me in that text.

"The preacher began thus: 'Dear friends, this is a very simple text, indeed. It says, "Look." Now looking don't take a deal of pains. It ain't liftin' your foot or your finger; it is just "look." Well, a man needn't go to college to learn to look. You may be the biggest fool, and yet you can look. A man needn't be worth a thousand a year to be able to look. Anyone can look; even a child can look. But then the text says, "Look unto *me.*" Ay!' said he in broad Essex, 'many on ye are lookin' to yourselves, but it's no use lookin' there. You'll never find any comfort in yourselves. Some look to God the Father. No, look to Him by-and-by. Jesus Christ says, "Look unto *Me.*" Some on ye say, "We must wait for the Spirit's workin'." You have no business with that just now. Look to Christ. The text says, "Look unto me."'

"Then the good man followed up his text in this way: 'Look unto Me; I am sweatin' great drops of blood. Look unto Me; I am hangin' on the cross. Look unto Me; I am dead and buried. Look unto Me; I rise again. Look unto Me; I ascend to heaven. Look unto

Me; I am sittin' at the Father's right hand. O poor sinner, look unto Me! Look unto ME!'

"When he had gone to about that length, and managed to spin out ten minutes or so, he was at the end of his tether. Then he looked at me under the gallery, and I dare say, with so few present, he knew me to be a stranger. Just fixing his eyes on me, as if he knew all my heart, he said, 'Young man, you look very miserable.' Well, I did, but I had not been accustomed to have remarks made from the pulpit on my personal appearance before. However, it was a good blow, struck right home. He continued, 'And you always will be miserable, miserable in life, and miserable in death—if you don't obey my text; but if you obey now, this moment, you will be saved.' Then, lifting up his hands, he shouted as only a primitive Methodist could do, 'Young man, look to Jesus Christ. Look! Look! Look! You have nothing to do but to look and live.'

"I saw at once the way of salvation. I know not what else he said—I did not take much notice of it—I was so possessed with that one thought. Like as when the brazen serpent was lifted up, the people only looked and were healed, so it was with me. I had been waiting to do fifty things, but when I heard that word, 'Look!' what a charming word it seemed to me! Oh! I looked until I could almost have looked my eyes away. There and then the cloud was gone, the darkness had rolled away, and that moment I saw the sun; and I could have risen that instant, and sung with the most enthusiastic of them, of the precious blood of Christ, and the simple faith which looks alone to Him. Oh, that somebody had told me this before. 'Trust Christ, and you shall be saved.'"—C. H. Spurgeon's *Autobiography,* pp. 105-107.

This same experience can be yours. "Look unto me, and be ye saved, all the ends of the earth" (Isa. 45:22).

Who Started

the

Whole Thing?

As one studies the first two chapters of Genesis, one question keeps finding its way into the mind: Why did Adam and Eve disobey God and start this whole thing called "sin"? There seems to be no reason for what they did.

The best way I know of to answer this question is to start at the very beginning—not Genesis 1:1, but even before that. If you add a column of figures wrong, there is only one way to get the right answer, and that is to start all over. It's no good to add the rest of the figures correctly unless the mistake has been found and taken care of. So we must go all the way back to the beginning to learn how sin began and who is responsible.

On November 7, 1940, the 5,979-foot, $6.4-million Tacoma Narrows Bridge collapsed into the Puget Sound in a "splash heard 'round the world." It had been completed only four months. When it was hit by a windstorm that reached over forty miles an hour the bridge convulsed, snapped apart, and plunged 190 feet into the water.

One engineer who worked on the bridge had repeatedly warned during its design and construction that flaws in its engineering would make it susceptible to certain kinds of forces—the very forces that later destroyed it. He had filed reports with the Government, but they were ignored. He had pleaded for additional supports to be added at strategic points, but in vain. Two days following the disaster he wrote to his son, "I have nothing to worry about, for I am covered by my reports on the bridge's condition from start to finish. I warned the Government over and over not to let the bridge be accepted prior to the satisfactory completion of measures to guard against the very conditions that have occurred. I am not responsible for the wrecking of this most beautiful span."

One thing we must ever keep in mind as we go back to the beginnings of sin: God is not responsible for the mess the human race is in. We cannot accuse Him of erroneous engineering or faulty planning. The record says, "And God saw every thing that he had made, and, behold, it was very good" (Gen. 1:31). He made all things, animate and inanimate, absolutely perfect.

When I say He made "all things," I include much more than this little planet and everything connected with it. God is the Creator of the entire universe and all the inhabitants of other worlds and planets. Those who believe in God are not the only ones who are quite certain that there is life, and lots of it, on other worlds. A host of atheists, evolutionists, and nonreligious people are equally sure.

If you ever visit the Air and Space Museum in Washington, D.C., be sure to relax in one of the large reclining chairs in the planetarium room and watch the spectacular night sky scenes projected on the vast concave ceiling. Listen carefully to the narration. You would think the scriptwriter had actually met beings from other planets, so confidently does he speak of extraterrestrial life. Eminent scientists firmly believe that the man who does not believe in life on other worlds is simply an egotistical earthling. Recent spacecraft, on interplanetary exploration, have carried special plaques mounted conspicuously on the exterior to communicate information about earth through diagrams and symbols that scientists hope intelligent life on other worlds might comprehend. Speaking of the boundless universe, Tennyson wrote, "Think you this world of hope and fears could find no statelier than his peers in yonder hundred million spheres?"

The Bible says much about orders of supernatural beings, created by God, which are all superior to man. Paul refers to "the whole family in heaven and earth" (Eph. 3:15). Some of these supernatural, nonterrestrial beings are usually referred to as angels. But please understand that nowhere in the Bible can one find any reference to angels being spirits or souls of dead people. This idea was concocted in the Middle Ages when religious superstitions, part of the mark-of-the-beast system, often smothered beautiful truths of Scripture. The Bible speaks of angels as created beings. God created them just as He did all things. "Praise him, all his angels. . . . For he commanded, and they were created" (Ps. 148:2-5). The Bible hints at different orders and ranks of angels—cherubim and seraphim. They are powerful and intelligent. They "excel in strength" (Ps. 103:20). One angel single-handedly slew 185,000 Assyrian soldiers (see 2

Kings 19:35). One "opened the prison doors" and delivered the apostles from prison (Acts 5:19). Thus the Bible indicates that the visible and the invisible world are in very close contact and that angels are very much involved with the affairs of men.

The problem is that not all the multitudes of angels (and there is an innumerable host of them, according to Daniel 7:10 and Revelation 5:11) are loyal to God. Since they are intelligent beings, they too were given freedom of choice by their Creator, and one of them perverted that freedom. Using interesting language, the prophet Ezekiel speaks of this one superb angel falling into sin. The prophet calls him "the model of perfection, full of wisdom and perfect in beauty." He was "anointed as a guardian cherub" and walked "on the holy mount of God." He was "blameless . . . from the day . . . [he was] created till wickedness was found in . . . [him]" (Eze. 28:12-15, N.I.V.).

Who was this exalted angel who perverted the freedom given him by God? How did it happen? One Bible translation refers to him as Lucifer, a Latin word meaning "light bearer" that reflects the high position he held before he sinned and was cast out of heaven. The prophet Isaiah describes in amazement the fall of this brilliant being. "How are you fallen from heaven, O Day Star, son of Dawn! How you are cut down to the ground, you who laid the nations low! You said in your heart, 'I will ascend to heaven; above the stars of God I will set my throne on high; I will sit on the mount of assembly in the far north; I will ascend above the heights of the clouds, I will make myself like the Most High'" (Isa. 14:12-14, R.S.V.). Apparently Lucifer, in

67

some mysterious, unexplained manner, became dissatisfied with his position as the highest of angels and aspired jealously to the position of God Himself.

One wonders how it was possible for God's *highest* created being, Lucifer, to become Satan, the deceiver of the universe. How could he have chosen to be anything less than perfect? Indeed, the failure of Lucifer—since he lived in the presence of the great Creator, in heaven itself, with no one and no thing to tempt him to sin—is less explainable than the failure of Adam. Neither Adam nor Lucifer was created with any disposition toward evil. God did not make them defective. Both were created with holy natures, without a trace of selfishness or sin in their minds.

The origin of sin is a mystery; there is no rational explanation for it. We can only come to the conclusion that sin was self-originated. But why? Perhaps C. S. Lewis' conjecture is the most plausible: "The moment you have a self at all, there is a possibility of putting yourself first." And that is exactly what Lucifer did and what he persuaded our first parents to do, too. Certainly there was no deficiency in God's divine government to cause his fall.

But in a paradoxical way the fact that sin does exist proves that God is a God of love. For He ran a risk in giving all intelligent created beings the freedom of choice. In no way would God force His beings to serve Him. His heart of love finds joy only in the response of willing obedience on the part of those who love Him. Thus God *could* have created a universe in which sin was impossible, but divine love would not allow Him to do so.

When Satan rebelled "he was cast out into the earth, and his angels were cast out with him" (Rev. 12:9). Tragically, many of the angels decided in favor of Satan's opposition to God's government and cast their lot with him. It seems incredible that both Satan and the angels that followed him could be so blinded to the terrible results of their actions. That is the reason sin—lawlessness and rebellion—is called a "mystery," or "secret" (see 2 Thess. 2:7).

Sin blinds the mind and causes irrational actions. Man does mysterious things under its influence. Have you ever said, "I can't figure out why she did that," or "It's unbelievably shocking what he did," or "It's beyond me why that family acts the way they do"? Think of all the materials designed by various groups to warn youth of the consequences if they get involved in drugs; yet thousands still plunge headlong into the drug scene. It is a mystery, isn't it? Adults, too, indulge in self-destructive behavior in spite of knowing the dangers—smoking, alcohol use, et cetera. Why? There is no good answer except to say that sin just doesn't make sense. The closest we can come to understanding its bewitching nature is to know the story of how it started in the universe and on our planet and what its basic ingredient is.

Isaiah's comment about the fall of Lucifer indicates that before any outward sin was evident there first developed an *inward* attitude of evil. The statement "You said in your heart" gives us a clue to the nature of sin. Sin is a disposition of the mind, an attitude of the soul. When you see an evil act, remember that the act is merely the fruit of an internal condition. Johnny is not bad because he steals; he steals because he is bad. Mary is not bad because she lies; she lies because she is bad. This doesn't mean that stealing and lying are not bad. They definitely are! But behind every *act* of sin is an underlying state of sinfulness. In other words, sinners sin because they are sinners; they are not sinners because they sin! They have a sinner's nature, and it becomes evident in the way they act. The outward actions are first in the inward mind. And all of us are born with this sinful nature. We sin easily and naturally. If every person were held accountable for his inward thoughts, there isn't a person living who would not deserve to be hanged!

At the very core of the mark-of-the-beast principle is—sin! Rebellion! Self-exaltation! Another symbol for the beast power is found in Revelation 17, where a dissolute woman rides a scarlet-colored beast. It is significant that written on her forehead is the word *mystery*. Here is a power that rebels against God, and "mystery" or "sin" is inscribed on its forehead. Notice in Revelation 14, which we have briefly discussed, that those who follow God have the Lamb's name and His Father's name written on *their* foreheads. This, too, is a mystery, and it is a far greater mystery than sin. "Beyond all question, the mystery of godliness is great" (1 Tim. 3:16, N.I.V.). Again the contrast is drawn, and we see the two groups—one loyal and the other disloyal. One group rebels, the other obeys. One group is possessed by the mystery of sin and the other by the mystery of godliness. One bears the mark of the beast on their foreheads; the other carries the seal of God.

In concluding this discussion on man's nature, let me direct your attention to what Christ has to say on the subject. Christ knew more about the nature of man than anyone else. "He did not need man's testimony about man, for he knew what was in a man" (John 2:25, N.I.V.). Jesus tried to show His hearers that sin comes from the inside out. Remember the word *heart* in Scripture usually refers to the mind. Jesus declared, "'For out of the heart come evil thoughts, murder, adultery, sexual immorality, theft, false testimony, slander'" (Matt. 15:19, N.I.V.).

On another occasion the Saviour very skillfully used a dishwashing illustration to make the same point. He said, "'You clean the outside of the cup and dish, but inside they are full of greed and self-indulgence'" (chap. 23:25, N.I.V.). Then to drive home His point more forcefully He continued, "'In the same way, on the outside you appear to people as righteous but on the inside you are full of hypocrisy and wickedness'" (verse 28, N.I.V.). His solution? "'First clean the inside of the cup and dish, and then the outside also will be clean'" (verse 26, N.I.V.).

Using yet another illustration, Jesus asked His enemies an embarrassing question: "'You brood of vipers, how can you who are evil say anything good?'" (chap. 12:34, N.I.V.). He added, "'For out of the overflow of the heart the mouth speaks.'" In this same passage Jesus sets forth an orderly progression that exists in the world of nature. "'Make a tree good and its fruit will be good, or make a tree bad and its fruit will be bad'" (verse 33, N.I.V.).

As in the world of nature, so it is in the spiritual

world. The inner nature, the roots, must be changed before the outside is truly changed. This change is the central theme of the seal-of-God principle. Before a person can be a citizen of the kingdom of God, he must experience this change! God puts His seal, His stamp of approval, only on the person who allows Him to make this change in the life. The mark-of-the-beast principle offers a person salvation without his having to change.

The fall of Lucifer because of his unwillingness to change his attitude to God's love has been reflected in the experience of his human followers through the centuries since Eden. As we will see in the next chapter, dealing with the second angel's message, those who have followed Satan's leading have fallen along with him, resulting in the angel's announcement of the collapse of "Babylon," which represents apostate religion.

The Fall

of

Babylon

Another angel, a second, followed, saying, 'Fallen, fallen is Babylon the great, she who made all nations drink the wine of her impure passion'" (Rev. 14:8, R.S.V.).

That's all the second angel said. But to John the words carried a world of meaning. To us, "Babylon" doesn't mean very much. If anything, it recalls a vague impression of ancient history we picked up somewhere. Of course, Babylon *is* ancient history. But that doesn't mean it isn't interesting and important, for these three messages, as previously pointed out, are the final messages of God to mankind before Jesus comes.

To John the word *Babylon* meant a great deal. He was a Hebrew and thoroughly familiar with the Old Testament Scriptures and the history of his people. Immediately his mind must have gone back to Babylon's role as related to Israel.

To a Jewish mind such as John's, Babylon stood for evil. Founded by Noah's great-grandson Nimrod, Babylon was the world's first city-kingdom (see Gen. 10:9, 10). The earliest recorded enterprise of this kingdom was an act of rebellion against God. The

Babylonians decided that they would build a tremendous tower so high it would reach into the very clouds of heaven itself (see chap. 11:1-9). The advantages of such a tower were obvious. If God should send another flood upon the earth, they could escape by climbing to the top of the tower. Of course, God had promised them that never again would another worldwide flood destroy every living thing. He had even pointed to the rainbow that appeared after each shower as proof of His promise. But they didn't trust Him. This point is significant: Babylon began in distrust of God.

Besides, by being able to ascend into the clouds, no doubt their scientists could determine just what had caused the Flood that Great-grandfather Noah had survived. And once they knew how God did it, it should be easy to control future floods He might send. Thus the beginnings of Babylon were steeped in opposition to God.

A careful reading of Genesis 11:4 gives an additional insight into the reasons these early dwellers of Babel had for building their tower. "Let us make a name for ourselves" (R.S.V.). Their tower was to capture the admiration of the world and demonstrate their self-sufficiency. Thus we see that to John the early history of Babylon would suggest the rebellion, distrust, and independence from God exhibited by the tower builders. It is interesting to note that all through the Scriptures God has attempted to show self-sufficient, sinful man that eternal things are in *His* hands, not in man's. The second angel's message is designed to impress again on man's mind the futility of human pride, boastfulness, and achievements.

By their presumptuous tower the Babylonians shook their fists at God, determined to defy Him and become a mighty power independent of Him. But God scattered them by confusing their language, and because of this the Hebrews identified the name Babylon with a word that meant *confusion.* The Babylonians themselves, however, attributed the name to a word in their own language, meaning "the gate of the gods." So rebellion against God marked the very beginning of Babylon.

Throughout the Old Testament history of God's dealings with men, Babylon appears as the main enemy of His people, the Israelites. Other nations attacked and harassed Israel, but it was Babylon who subjugated God's people completely and carried practically the entire population into captivity.

In no uncertain terms Isaiah names Satan as the unseen agent who controlled Babylon. "Thou shalt take up this proverb against the king of Babylon, and say, How hath the oppressor ceased! the golden city ceased!" "How art thou fallen from heaven, O Lucifer, son of the morning! how art thou cut down to the ground, which didst weaken the nations!" (Isa. 14:4, 12).

You see, Babylon was Satan's Old Testament counterpart, or counterfeit, for God's people. He knew that God intended to use the Israelites as His special representatives on earth. So Satan determined to have a particular group of people through whom he could work. Babylon stands throughout the Bible as a symbol of the forces of Satan, which oppose God and

His chosen people.

God did everything He could to enable Israel to fulfill His purposes. He worked impressive miracles for them; He gave them His law and committed to them the privilege of sharing His love to the rest of the world.

But, unfortunately, Israel as a whole failed God. Its history may be seen as an up-and-down experience of prevailing unfaithfulness relieved by only occasional periods of obedience. At last, because of continual apostasy, God removed His protecting shield from His people, and Babylon, spurred on by Satan, attacked Jerusalem and carried most of the Hebrews into captivity. God hoped this drastic measure would shock His chosen people into realizing their sin and cause them to turn to Him in faith. Through the prophets He told the Israelites the reason for their captivity. He urged them to repent, and He declared that Babylon, too, would receive the sure results of her wicked course. He even predicted how long their captivity in Babylon would last—seventy years. (See Dan. 9:2; Jer. 25:12.)

Anticipating the close of the seventy years, God, through Jeremiah, called His people out of Babylon. "'Flee from the midst of Babylon, let every man save his life! Be not cut off in her punishment, for this is the time of the Lord's vengeance'" (Jer. 51:6, R.S.V.). "'Go out of the midst of her, my people!'" (verse 45, R.S.V.).

But only a small group of approximately fifty thousand Hebrews returned to Israel. The great majority preferred to stay in the land that for seventy years had been their home.

God also declared through His prophets that total destruction would come to Babylon as a result of her sins. "'She shall be peopled no more for ever, nor inhabited for all generations. As when God overthrew Sodom and Gomorrah and their neighbor cities, says the Lord, so no man shall dwell there'" (chap. 50:39, 40, R.S.V.).

The word of God proved true, for the Median and Persian armies conquered Babylon, and eventually the kingdom lay in desolate ruins, never to be rebuilt. This beautiful city with its yellow-brick outer walls, blue gates, rose-red palaces, and glistening white temples became a desolate ruin. Its bricks were used to build other cities at different sites.

Satan had designed that Babylon should be the nerve center for his master plan of deceiving the whole world and leading it into opposition to God, whose temple was at Jerusalem. These two cities, in Old Testament times, became symbolic of the forces of evil on the one hand and the forces of righteousness on the other. Babylon's wealth and power seemed so stable that none dreamed it would ever fall. And when it did, the world never forgot it. The shock of Babylon's fall and the loss of its power, importance, and beauty still impressed men in John's day, some six hundred years later.

So when John heard the second of the three angels shout, "Fallen, fallen is Babylon the great," he knew that the angel was not referring to the physical kingdom of ancient Babylon, for that city lay in desolate ruins. He realized that God was using the term "Babylon" as a symbol of the wicked forces that would be in opposition to God's people in the final days of earth, just as ancient Babylon had tried to destroy God's people in Old Testament times. And these forces of evil would be *religious forces*.

Notice that John heard the angel identify Babylon as "she who made all nations drink the wine of her impure passion" (Rev. 14:8, R.S.V.). The King James Version of the Bible translates this verse: "She made all nations drink of the wine of the wrath of her fornication."

God, you see, symbolizes His relationship with His people by the closest earthly union two people can know—marriage. He says, "For thy Maker is thine husband; the Lord of hosts is his name" (Isa. 54:5). Paul declares of the church, "I betrothed you to Christ to present you as a pure bride to her one husband" (2 Cor. 11:2, R.S.V.).

Adultery means unfaithfulness to marriage vows. It destroys the close union between husband and wife that has been pledged. That's why God uses the terms "fornication" or "adultery" to represent spiritual unfaithfulness, which destroys the "marriage relationship" that He wants to have with His people.

So Babylon, who had caused the nations to drink the wine of her impure passion (meaning to unite with her in adultery or apostasy from God), must be a symbol of false religion that draws men away from God. Since these angels of Revelation 14 deliver their messages in the days just prior to the return of Jesus, Babylon must represent the apostate, false religious forces that oppose God and His faithful people just before the Second Coming.

In fact, Revelation 17:4-6 specifically points to Babylon as a symbol of apostate religions. In vision John saw a woman with the name written in her forehead: "'Babylon the great, mother of harlots and of earth's abominations'" (verse 5, R.S.V.). He says she was drunk on the blood of the saints and martyrs of Jesus. These words must refer to a religious power that persecutes the saints of God.

But John heard the angel announcing the *fall* of this symbolic Babylon. What is the fall of Babylon? How does she fall?

In a previous chapter we saw that the great theme running through all three of the angels' messages (and throughout all of Scripture) is the concept of a mighty struggle, or controversy, between Satan and Jesus Christ, between a false gospel, based on human achievement, and God's genuine gospel of salvation by faith in the merits of Jesus. The history of Babylon began with this same attitude by the tower builders of independence from God and reliance on human achievement.

Later, Nebuchadnezzar, the king of Babylon who took the Hebrews captive, did likewise. Refusing to recognize God's power, he took to himself the credit for all his exploits and achievements. "Is not this great Babylon," he said, "that I have built for the house of the kingdom by the might of my power, and for the honour of my majesty?" (Dan. 4:30). As a result, Nebuchadnezzar lost his reason for seven years, after which he was willing to extol the God of heaven. This same spirit of self-sufficiency is at the root of the false gospel that Satan attempts to substitute for the genuine.

It was this desire to be independent of God and to control his own existence apart from God that caused Lucifer's fall in heaven and turned him into Satan. It was the same attitude that caused the fall of the tower at the very beginning of Babylon's history. It was the same attitude that caused Nebuchadnezzar's fall and later the fall of his kingdom under Belshazzar. And it is the same attitude of self-sufficiency and salvation apart from God that causes symbolic Babylon's fall at the end of time. The same identical power—Satan—has been behind Babylon in each of its phases.

John heard the angel say that Babylon falls "because she made all nations drink of the wine of the wrath of her fornication." Thus the angel indicates that Babylon will initiate an incestuous relationship with the nations, or political organizations, of the earth. She will cause them to drink the wine of her fornication, indicating her efforts to secure support for her false gospel.

This, too, is mirrored in ancient Babylon. There the might and power of the state were arrayed to force conformity to religious beliefs and practices. Nebuchadnezzar commanded all his subjects, including the captive Hebrews, to worship a great golden image he had erected. The penalty for refusal was death (see Daniel 3). So with the union of political power and apostate religious forces at the end of time. This union will try to coerce those who want to remain faithful to God to join in spiritual adultery by disobeying God's commandments. By her efforts to force disobedience to God and loyalty to the beast power, Babylon receives her final fall.

In Revelation 18:1 John sees a mighty angel who floods the earth with its glory. This angel represents a combination of all three of the angels of Revelation 14. John hears this mighty angel repeat the announcement of Babylon's fall and give the reason for it: "For all nations have drunk of the wine of the wrath of her fornication, and the kings of the earth have committed fornication with her, and the merchants of the earth are waxed rich through the abundance of her delicacies" (Rev. 18:2, 3).

This additional verse brings to view a worldwide union of religious, political, and economic institutions in a great conspiracy of evil designed to crush the faithful people of God. Revelation 13 points to a similar situation, declaring that a sentence of death (just as in ancient Babylon under Nebuchadnezzar) will be levied against all those who refuse to fall into step with this powerful coalition (see verse 15).

Just as God's Old Testament people faced death and destruction by the literal kingdom of Babylon, so God's last-day people will face death and destruction by spiritual or symbolic Babylon. But God intervened in behalf of His people back then, and He will do the same in the future.

Babylon fell as a literal kingdom when Cyrus, a Persian general, overthrew the city. But the fall of spiritual Babylon is a moral fall as well as a physical collapse. The physical fall of spiritual Babylon takes place in connection with the second coming of Jesus (see 2 Thess. 1:7-9; Rev. 16:17-21; 18:8-24). God's justice will destroy those who have willfully rebelled against Him. At this time the forces of religious apostasy will receive their just reward from heaven. But the reason for Babylon's physical destruction lies in her moral fall.

This moral fall consists of her rebellious adultery in allying herself with civil authority and economic influences against truth and in her consistent opposition to God and His gracious gospel. The crowning act that finalizes her moral fall and brings about her physical destruction is her persecution to the death of God's faithful followers. The decree will go forth that those who persist in "stubbornly" accepting the grace of God by faith in Jesus Christ for salvation and who continue to show their loyalty to God by their obedience to His commandments deserve to die. By this act Babylon will completely cut herself off from God and ensure her final ruin.

In its simplest form, then, "Babylon is fallen" means spiritual confusion. No doubt the Christians in John's day applied the title "Babylon" to imperial Rome, which mercilessly tortured and murdered the early Christians. Both symbolically and literally, Babylon has been traditionally recognized as the enemy of God's truth and His people. Thus, as it is used in the second angel's message, this name becomes symbolic of all apostate religious organizations, whether Christian or non-Christian.

John heard a voice from heaven appealing to the loyal minority of earth to separate themselves from this renegade religious power. "And I heard another voice from heaven, saying, Come out of her my people, that ye be not partakers of her sins, and that ye receive not of her plagues" (Rev. 18:4).

God's appeal today to you is: "Come out of falsehood and take your stand on the side of right. Babylon is falling, and her sins are mounting up to heaven. Soon she will collapse from the weight of her errors and receive the punishment she so richly deserves. Come out of her while you can!"

Babylon holds a golden cup to the lips of kings and merchants, enticing them to drink and unite with her in rebellion against God's truth (chap. 17:4). But God also holds a cup; it is filled with the fierceness of His wrath against sin. John saw that "Babylon came in remembrance before God, to give unto her the cup of the wine of the fierceness of his wrath" (chap. 16:19). God must punish sin; Babylon will be destroyed, and so will everyone who follows her false gospel in defiance of God's gracious offers of mercy. That is why God pleads with human beings to come out now while there is time, and separate themselves from Babylon's errors and confusion.

Not many will respond to God's call. Only a small remnant of the Hebrews returned to Judah from Babylon at the close of the seventy years of captivity. History has always recorded that only a small number, compared to the vast majority, have followed right-eousness and loyalty to God. So in the spiritual captivity of the last days, only a few will listen to God's appeal and come out of Babylon, taking their place fearlessly on the side of God and truth.

But to those who do, God will give the righteous-ness of Jesus to cover their sins. They will receive forgiveness and peace and eternal life with God Himself.

Can we bear to apply the second angel's message a bit closer to our own personal lives? The second angel's message, when combined with the loud cry of the angel of Revelation 18, who calls for God's people to come out of Babylon, implies far more than changing church membership from one denomination to another. If a liar, a drunkard, or the sexually impure leaves one church merely to join another without a change of heart and actions, what good does it do?

The downfall of nations or organizations or religious systems is simply the combined downfall of individuals. Churches are composed of people. There is really no difference between the principles that bring about the collective downfall of a vast organization and those affecting an individual fall.

Did you ever stop to think that an individual spiritual downfall is guaranteed for each of us at birth? Didn't David exclaim, "Behold, I was shapen in iniquity; and in sin did my mother conceive me" (Ps. 51:5)? Didn't Paul emphasize this unwelcome truth in Romans 8:3 by using the term "sinful flesh"? In fact, he goes so far as to say, "For to be carnally [fleshly] minded is death; but to be spiritually minded is life and peace" (verse 6). These terms—"in sin," "carnally minded"—describe the state of fallen Babylon. They also describe our natural human condition apart from the saving knowledge of God's grace through Jesus Christ our Saviour.

Praise God for the second angel's message, which is one of tremendous hope! Connected with the appeal of Revelation 18:4—"Come out of her, my people"—it is a wonderful promise of assurance that when we are willing to set aside our natural self-sufficiency and pride to give our wills to God, our lives will be "lightened with his glory" (verse 1).

There is no way out of the dilemma caused by our naturally sinful state except to receive by faith the gracious provisions God has supplied. The apostle Paul declares, "For all have sinned, and come short of the glory of God," but he adds in the very next verse, "Being justified freely by his grace through the redemption that is in Christ Jesus" (Rom. 3:23, 24). "For God so loved the world, that he gave his only begotten Son, that whosoever believeth in him should not perish, but have everlasting life" (John 3:16).

There can be no compromise between the mark-of-the-beast principle, in which man is his own savior and depends on no one outside himself, and the seal-of-God principle, in which man recognizes his helplessness to overcome sin and trusts wholly on the merits of the Saviour provided as a free gift by God. It is this counterfeit gospel, the mark-of-the-beast principle, that permeates Babylon and causes its great fall.

The cross of Christ stands at dead center in the second angel's message. To come out of Babylon is not easy. It means a death to self. The cross stands for death; the second angel's message declares that we must die to the Babylonian principle of self-rule and in its stead place the Creator of heaven and earth as the ruler of our being.

Those who come out of Babylon by placing their faith in Christ will find the wonderful promise of forgiveness and eternal life fulfilled. As God said through Jeremiah to the little group of Hebrews who went back to Judah from Babylonian captivity: "'In those days and in that time, says the Lord, iniquity shall be sought in Israel, and there shall be none; and sin in Judah, and none shall be found; for I will pardon those whom I leave as a remnant'" (Jer. 50:20, R.S.V.). What a beautiful picture of the experience that may be ours! What a contrast to the awful doom pronounced upon those who worship the beast and receive his mark! However, even amid the severity of God's wrath against the beast and its followers can be discerned a positive message of courage, hope, and salvation, as we shall see in the next chapter.

Trash or Trees,
Cans or Clouds,
Bottles or Birds?

My wife and I live in a country setting, so often we take walks. I used to get quite perturbed over the numerous cans and bottles that people threw out of their cars, littering the roadside. (By the way, I've noticed that about 99 percent of the cans and bottles are beer and liquor containers. I rarely see any milk, juice, or soft-drink containers. Draw your own conclusions!) This constant cluttering of the roads bothered me almost to the extent that I failed to enjoy the trees, skies, clouds, birds, and wildflowers. The bottles, cans, and other trash absorbed my attention. Trash, not trees; cans, not clouds; bottles, not birds; waste, not wildflowers, captured my thoughts and made me angry.

This experience has taught me a lesson. No longer do I let the roadside garbage mar my walks. Of course, I still feel disgusted at those thoughtless litterers who certainly should know better. But this disgust no longer outweighs the joy of walking and communing with my Lord through nature.

So it is in the spiritual realm. Now, when I use the term "spiritual realm" I do not intend to divide life into parts. Life is indivisible, and man is a total package of mind, body, and spirit. What affects one part affects the other, either for good or ill. For instance, a converted Christian will not desecrate God's landscape with his trash! When a person has a union with Christ, his entire life style is transformed. But the point I'm making underscores the theme of looking to Jesus. When the Saviour is lifted up in our thoughts, when we fasten our eyes of faith upon Him instead of upon the garbage around us in the world, then something begins to happen to us!

What causes us to look to Jesus? My only answer is, the working of the Holy Spirit, the third person of the Godhead. This is the very first step toward salvation. Nothing precedes it. I cannot even desire to look to Jesus unless the Spirit leads me to. I cannot repent or change unless the Spirit brings me to it. So the very first step toward Jesus is taken through the drawing power of God's Holy Spirit. Then as we respond and yield to this drawing, we move toward Jesus, which in turn causes us to repent. Those who believe that they must repent *before* they come to Jesus are making a serious mistake. If this could be done, then we wouldn't need the Saviour. The fact is that no man, by his own decision or will, can repent, nor can he make himself worthy of the blessings of forgiveness that we call justification.

I must run the risk of wearying you by repeating that salvation is *God's* work, not man's! This is why it is termed salvation through faith alone in Jesus Christ. This is the heart of the seal-of-God principle. The mark-of-the-beast principle is that man can save himself, or at the very least do something that will get him to heaven and make him acceptable to God. It is a hateful, despicable counterfeit of God's true plan of salvation. Furthermore, it is an insult to God to try to buy one's way into the kingdom when He has offered it as a gift, at the enormous price of the life, death, resurrection, and high priestly ministry of His Son, Jesus Christ.

When the Holy Spirit touches our hearts and impresses us to look to Jesus, we will be drawn to Him if we do not consciously resist. We have a choice of rejecting or accepting this wooing of the Holy Spirit; we can passively neglect or we can yield to His pleadings. Probably the majority of those who will never experience salvation will be those who passively neglect God's call through the Holy Spirit. But whether we reject or neglect, the result is the same—we are lost! "How shall we escape if we ignore such a great salvation?" (Heb. 2:3, N.I.V.).

The Holy Spirit must be permitted to intrude, if you please, into the inner sanctum of our minds and break the obsessive hold of selfishness, self-preservation, and self-gratification, while pointing our eyes to the uplifted Christ on the cross. It is while looking to Jesus that we see God, who became a flesh-and-blood member of our lost race, living and dying as man's substitute. We see "that God was reconciling the world to himself in Christ, not counting men's sins against them" (2 Cor. 5:19, N.I.V.). We see God as a man among men, by His perfect life settling forever the immutability of heaven's precepts and completely fulfilling the law's requirements on man's behalf. Finally, we see God shedding His blood to pay the full price for our sins, the penalty justice demanded. "Christ redeemed us from the curse of the law by becoming a curse for us" (Gal. 3:13, N.I.V.).

When the sinner, through the leading of the Holy Spirit, begins to understand what the Saviour has done for him, he experiences what we term "repentance." His heart cries out with those who on the Day of Pentecost were convicted by the Spirit-filled preaching of Peter, "What shall . . . [I] do?" Peter's immediate answer to the crowd is valid for us today. "Repent" (Acts 2:37, 38). And again, what leads to repentance? Our own decision? No! "The goodness of God leadeth thee to repentance" (Rom. 2:4). Do you see the principle involved here? You must first be drawn to the Saviour, and when you see His goodness, His perfect love, *then* you repent. But you can never properly repent until you sense the righteousness, the goodness, the unutterable kindness and love of God. In repenting you experience a deep sorrow for your sins. This deep sorrow turns you against sin. Then the Holy Spirit creates in your heart a truly deep desire to be clean, to be pure, to be restored to a close fellowship with Jesus.

Perhaps the finest example of true repentance in Scripture is that of King David, who committed the double crime of murder and adultery. His great prayer of repentance is found in Psalm 51. I have memorized it, and I urge you to memorize it, too. David begs God for mercy; he acknowledges his sins; he pleads for cleansing; he beseeches God to create in him a clean heart and to renew a right spirit within him. He appeals for the presence of the Holy Spirit to remain with him and asks for restoration of the joy of salvation. Finally, David proclaims the goodness of God and His righteousness. Take your Bible, and on your knees study this psalm reverently. Ask God to do for you what He did for David. You may not have gone so far as to murder and commit adultery, but *any* sin can destroy your relationship with the Lord. Remember, in asking the Lord for this kind of repentance, that it is beyond the reach of your own power to produce. It comes strictly as a gift from God. Don't procrastinate. If God is speaking through His Spirit to your heart right now, please surrender yourself to Him and say, "Lord, I see what a terrible sinner I am, but I thank You for being such a wonderful Saviour to accept me. Please forgive me and create in me a clean heart and renew a right spirit within me. I believe You will do this for me."

If you sincerely pray a prayer similar to this, what do you think the Lord will do? Perhaps the words of Jesus are the best answer. "If a son shall ask bread of any of you that is a father, will he give him a stone? or if he ask a fish, will he for a fish give him a serpent?" (Luke 11:11). What a wonderful Lord we are dealing with! He is so wonderful that He legally forgave the human race for all their sins even before Adam and Eve sinned. It is almost unbelievable that Christ is "the Lamb slain from the foundation of the world" (Rev. 13:8). Quite apart from man's wisdom, ability, and consent, God reconciled the whole human race to Himself through forgiveness, or what is termed justification. It is amazing that God has taken the initiative for reconciling us to Himself when we are the cause of the ruptured relationship to begin with! What does this say to you? It says that God loves you and me beyond belief. God wants you and me with Him forever. If He didn't, He would not have sent His Son on such an expensive journey to save us. Because of His infinite, reconciling love, God could *legally* save the whole human race in the righteousness of its substitute, Jesus Christ, but He will never destroy our freedom to choose. At this juncture we must be very careful not to fall into the trap of universalism, which teaches that everyone is ultimately saved because God has legally justified and reconciled all mankind.

A well-known illustration will appropriately underscore the point. A person is in debt a million dollars and has no way of paying it. But a very rich friend learns of his predicament and deposits a million dollars to the debtor's checking account to be used in paying the debt. The debtor must, of his own volition, accept or reject the gift; it is up to him. If he chooses not to accept the gift, he is still a million dollars in debt, even though the provision for payment has been made in full and deposited to his account.

So the good news is that Christ has paid our debt without any work or action on our part. By that I mean that nothing you can do will cancel even the smallest sin you have committed. I once was holding a series of religious meetings on the beautiful island of Penang, off the west coast of Malaysia. We were talking in those meetings of salvation and repentance. A wealthy gentleman attended my meetings and invited me to visit with him in his palatial home.

After talking on various subjects, he finally said,

"I've been listening to your lectures and was interested in the point you made that nothing I do can cancel my sins. The only way, you claim, for sin to be forgiven, is to accept what Christ has done. But," he continued, "I don't accept your thesis. In my younger years I did a lot of foolish things, but now that I am rich and older I have used my wealth to help the poor and to contribute to worthy causes. I believe my youthful acts of evil are now paid for by the good deeds that I have performed since I am older."

No amount of persuasion could change this man's mind. He tenaciously held to his belief in salvation by works.

There are a thousand subtle ways for this "works principle" to become a part of our everyday life. Even the performance of some kind deed to a person in need gives us a sense of satisfaction, and it should. But do not let it ever lead you to think that these actions give you credit in heaven for salvation. A husband can heap gifts on his wife but then turn around and abuse her verbally and emotionally, thinking in his heart that he has a right to do so since he has given her so much.

This salvation-by-works syndrome rears its ugly head in all facets of life. Did you ever hear someone say, "Well, I'm just as good as Joe, and even though I don't go to church I'll get to heaven if he does"? This, too, is part of salvation by works and the mark-of-the-beast principle.

We must learn and believe beyond the shadow of a doubt that salvation is of the Lord. It is what *Christ* has done and is doing for us that saves us. *He* is the one to get all the praise and the honor and the glory for having provided our salvation.

In our spiritual experience we need to look up—not to the trash, cans, and bottles. Keep the eyes focused on Jesus and know that all the benefits of salvation originate with Him, not with self.

Is
the War
Over?

Several years ago a homeowner on the Pacific island of Guam went out in his back yard early in the morning just in time to see a strange, rag-covered creature scurry with fright back into the jungle. When captured a few hours later, the creature turned out to be a Japanese soldier, half-dressed in the tattered remains of a uniform! His hair was long and matted; his malnourished, emaciated body was covered with scars. For twenty-five years, since the end of World War II on September 2, 1945, he had lived more like an animal than a human being, hiding in the jungle.

Why, since the war was over, did he live under such frightful and appalling conditions? The truth is, this poor soldier *didn't know the war was over.* In fact, it was difficult to persuade him of that fact. I have often wondered how he felt after returning to Japan and falling into the arms of his loved ones and relatives. How do you suppose he felt when he thought of the twenty-five horrible years he had lived under desperate, near-suicidal conditions, when he could have been safe and comfortable with his family at home? Do you suppose he ever became upset to think that for all that time he had not known that peace had been declared between Japan and America?

This soldier's story is, in reality, the story of man today and of his ignorance of God's plan for reconciliation with human beings. Multitudes are wandering around in the jungles of sin, living under horrible conditions, not knowing that peace has been declared between God and man through the life, death, and resurrection of the Lord Jesus Christ. They don't know the message of salvation by faith alone in Jesus. They don't know that because of Heaven's priceless gift, Jesus, the war is over. Peace can be theirs, but they continue their fearful existence! The Saviour promised this marvelous peace to those who would accept it. "Peace I leave with you, my peace I give unto you: not as the world giveth, give I unto you." Then He added, "Let not your heart be troubled, neither let it be afraid" (John 14:27). The kind of peace Jesus offers is permanent. It is this peace that everyone desperately seeks and few really find, because they are looking for it in the wrong places.

The key to finding this permanent, satisfying peace lies in a single word. It is one that we have mentioned before, but it needs broader emphasis. That word is *justification*.

We use this word or its concept all the time in our ordinary speech but not so often in the context of salvation. In courts of law people are forever justifying their actions. "The reason I killed him is because . . ." "I exceeded the speed limit because . . ." "I left my husband because . . ." Every action we perform, we consciously or subconsciously try to justify. "I bought this particular car, washing machine, mixer, because

. . ." Whether our actions are good or bad, we go through life constantly trying to justify our words, feelings, and actions. The most depraved criminals do the same. Even Hitler had his reasons for slaughtering millions of Jews!

Not only do we justify self but in many instances we attempt to rectify a situation by some action on our part. Adam and Eve, after pioneering in sin, tried to justify themselves by blaming others for their error. Adam blamed Eve; Eve blamed the serpent; and ultimately both put the blame on God. Here we see the first justifying attempt in human history. Then to cover their nakedness—symbolically representing their sin, for sin stripped man of his righteousness—they created their own robe of leaves to cover themselves. Here is the first attempt to rectify—or to pay for, if you please—human wrongdoing. And ever since, man has been trying to justify and rectify his mistakes in the wrong way. This attitude is so deeply ingrained in us that it manifests itself in literally every segment of life. We can't even receive an invitation to dinner without the immediate reaction of planning to "pay it back" by inviting our hosts to a meal at *our* house in the future.

A man may mistreat his wife, saying unkind and cruel words. Later, he tries to make it up to her by buying candy, flowers, or some lovely gift. His despicable actions are supposedly justified by his gift-giving. In a more direct manner, religiously oriented people try to justify self and rectify their sins by giving offerings, attending church, studiously reading the Bible, lighting candles, making pilgrimages, torturing their bodies, enduring long fasts, serving in some church office. This is not to say, of course, that it is wrong to study the Bible or serve in a church office, but the motivation behind the action may be all wrong. It is our motive that determines what kind of act it is. But precious few people really stop to think why they do what they do. Indeed, it isn't at all easy to make such determinations. Jeremiah was quite aware of this: "The heart is deceitful above all things, and desperately wicked: who can know it?" (Jer. 17:9).

There is yet another horrible side effect to the problem of incorrectly settled sin. The reason man is constantly trying to justify himself by making excuses for his failures and paying for his faults is to free himself from guilt. The well-known psychiatrist Dr. Karl Menninger in his book *Whatever Became of Sin?* illustrates the problem with a story:

"On a sunny day in September, 1972, a stern-faced, plainly dressed man could be seen standing still on a street corner in the busy Chicago Loop. As pedestrians hurried by on their way to lunch or business, he would solemnly lift his right arm, and pointing to the person nearest him intone loudly the single word 'GUILTY!'

"Then, without any change of expression, he would resume his stiff stance for a few moments before repeating the gesture. Then, again, the inexorable raising of his arm, the pointing, and the solemn pronouncing of the one word 'GUILTY!' "—Page 1. Menninger goes on to say that this strange action had an extraordinary effect on passing strangers. Many would hesitate, look at the strange man, then look away, and then at him again, then hurriedly continue on their way.

One man, turning to another who was Menninger's informant, exclaimed, "But how did *he* know?" Undoubtedly others had similar thoughts. How *did* he know, indeed?

"'Guilty!' *Everyone* guilty? Guilty of what? Guilty of overparking? Guilty of lying? Guilty of arrogance? Guilty of 'borrowing,' not to say embezzling? Guilty of unfaithfulness to a husband or wife? Guilty only of evil thoughts—or evil plans?"—Page 2.

The next question is, Guilty before whom? Policemen? friends? relatives? employers? God? whom?

We react to guilt by saying, "I can give it up." "I will give it back." "I will apologize." "I wasn't myself when I did that." "No one knows about it." "I'm going to quit." "I wouldn't want my family to see me." "How can I ever straighten it out?" "What's done can't be undone."

The problem of guilt is so massive that this entire volume could be dedicated to the causes and results of it. I am referring not only to guilt caused by sin. We suffer from guilt that in many cases is not directly related to the sin problem. Some workaholics can't sit down and relax five minutes without feeling guilty for being lazy! Even this type of guilt is part of the fruitage of the operation of the mark-of-the-beast principle. When a person experiences the peace that Jesus gives, sin-created and culture-created guilt is met resolutely and resolved.

When man first sinned, guilt immediately domi-

MARKED!

nated his feelings. This, in turn, motivated him to do something—anything—to escape these feelings of guilt. As a result, self-justification, excuses, rectification, attempts to repay, and such diversionary tactics as drugs (including alcohol), pleasures, and riotous living came in. These man-made "solutions" have the effect of modifying, quieting, and even eliminating temporarily, the screams of guilt. But such "peace" is an uneasy and short-lived one. That is why "'there is no rest [no peace] day or night for those who worship the beast . . . or for anyone who receives the mark of his name'" (Rev. 14:11, N.I.V.).

Man, in his natural state of enmity toward God, will find some means of solving the problem of guilt. Either he will adhere to a counterfeit system of justification (the mark-of-the-beast principle) by performing some penance to pay for his sin or he will plunge into a round of pleasure, work, sin, or some activity that will keep his conscience at bay. Ultimately, through repeated violations, he will eventually deaden his conscience until guilt is gone. The Scripture speaks of this condition as having one's conscience "seared with a hot iron" (1 Tim. 4:2).

We should clearly understand that if guilt is not dealt with adequately, it will eventually destroy us. Nothing is more wretched than the mind that is conscious of guilt. Unresolved guilt will ultimately destroy for eternity those who do not accept the Sinless One as the only genuine solution to the guilt problem. We cannot justify ourselves—only Jesus can. Sin has ruptured man's relationship with God. Justification, which Christ provides, is the primary means of restoring a right relationship with God. This justification can be equated with forgiveness. The most cheering words the human ear can hear are, "Your sins and your guilt are taken away."

The story of the paralyzed man in Capernaum is a wonderful illustration of God's release from guilt. Scripture does not tell us the man's name, but he was a hopeless case. His paralysis was horrible, yet his remorse and guilt over the life of sin he had lived (a life that undoubtedly brought about his physical condition) was slowly killing him. His helpless, hopeless condition drove him ever deeper into the clutches of despair. Then he began hearing of the wonderful works of Jesus. The stories of lepers being cured gave him hope, but then he thought of his own wickedness and feared that this marvelous Healer would condemn him. His fears drove him to despair. Finally, his desire to be free from his burden of guilt goaded him to persuade a few friends to carry him on his bed to the Saviour.

As they neared the house where Jesus was, crowds of people blocked all avenues of approach. Repeatedly the stretcher-bearers tried to push their way through to the Great Physician. Imagine the anguish of the paralytic, who had managed to get so near to the One who could solve his problems and yet was still so far away! Finally, they conceived the idea of taking him to the roof and removing enough tiles to make an opening his bed could fit through. What an amazing scene! Imagine the dust and debris floating down on Jesus and the people who were jammed in the house! First they see a hole being made in the roof, then a bed with ropes on each corner is lowered through the hole and comes to rest before the Saviour. What faith this sick man had!

Do you remember in an earlier chapter we discussed the marvelous truth that God makes the first step toward our salvation? So it was with this unfortunate paralytic. The Saviour had seen this man in his hovel long before he came for healing. Jesus Himself had brought conviction to his heart. Now, in great joy, the Saviour saw the fruition of that conviction.

As the emaciated victim lay at the feet of Jesus, one wonders what thoughts raced through His mind. The Saviour knew the greatest longing of his heart was not for physical healing but for spiritual ease, and He did not wait long to answer those longings. With tender love and care He said, " 'Son, your sins are forgiven' " (Mark 2:5, N.I.V.). Notice that Jesus forgave the man's sins *before* healing him. The number one problem of the diseased human race is the sin problem! Guilt resulting from sin is the greatest killer of all. Many are dying today of sickness and disease brought about by guilt and remorse. When this poor man heard these words of forgiveness, a mountainous burden rolled off his soul. He lay back in sweet peace. He, the guilty sinner, was pardoned! In childlike faith, he believed Jesus and was at peace.

Some of the church leaders watching this intriguing scene accused Jesus of blasphemy, because only God can forgive sins. Their accusations would have been in order had not Jesus been God the Son, who had every right to forgive sin. To prove to them this right, He spoke words of healing to the man. Immediately his disease was banished and, taking up his bed, he returned home rejoicing in both spiritual and physical health!

What a scene! What a Saviour! What a lesson for us today! Jesus forgave (justified) this sinner, not because of any works or restitution he had performed. This man experienced what the New Testament church eventually lost and Martin Luther rediscovered centuries later—God's redeeming grace apart from man's worthiness. It needs to be discovered individually by those who hope to enter heaven. How I wish every human being on earth would discover it and be saved!

When the great truth of justification by faith alone in Christ is lost sight of, man begins to invent ways and means of recommending himself to God, of getting to heaven by his own merits. Luther looked upon God as a severe judge, who must be placated by man's doings or works. For Luther the most terrifying word in Scripture was *righteousness,* because when he sensed his own sinfulness and compared it to the righteousness of God, he became overwhelmed with doubt and despair. His response was to exert himself to the utmost, performing penance and complying rigidly with every law the church commanded, in an effort to earn righteousness. Still he had no peace.

Luther lived in a day when the Bible was not studied to any great extent. So when he discovered Romans 1:16 and read, "The gospel . . . is the power of God unto salvation," it was a fresh revelation. Here was what Luther wanted. Like the paralytic, he

103

yearned for salvation! But when he came to verse 17, "For in the gospel a righteousness from God is revealed" (N.I.V.), he was thrown into deeper despair. He mistakenly believed that the Old Testament portrayed a God of vengeance and judgment, while the New Testament presented a different God. How could he ever reconcile the gospel with righteousness if righteousness meant judgment? If that were true, then the gospel would condemn and not save. Luther began to study, as never before, this subject of righteousness. He came to Romans 3:21, "But now a righteousness from God, *apart from law*, has been made known" (N.I.V.). Note the words "apart from law," or in other words, apart from works. No penance, no money, no pilgrimage, no performance of some duty could achieve this righteousness. Here was a righteousness Luther knew nothing about, although he himself was a church leader.

Luther describes his experience: "I greatly longed to understand Paul's Epistle to the Romans, and nothing stood in my way but that one expression, 'the justice (righteousness) of God,' because I took it to mean that justice whereby God is just and deals justly in punishing the unjust. My situation was that, although an impeccable monk, I stood before God as a sinner troubled in conscience, and I had no confidence that my merit would assuage Him. Therefore I did not love a just and angry God, but rather hated and murmured against Him. Yet I clung to the dear Paul and had a great yearning to know what he meant.

"Night and day I pondered until I saw the connection between the justice of God and the statement that 'the just shall live by his faith.' Then I grasped that the justice of God is that righteousness by which through grace and sheer mercy God justifies us through faith. Thereupon I felt myself to be reborn and to have gone through open doors into paradise. The whole of Scripture took on a new meaning, and whereas before 'the justice of God' had filled me with hate, now it became to me inexpressibly sweet in greater love. This passage of Paul became to me a gate of heaven."—Robert M. Horn, *Go Free* (Intervarsity Press), pp. 22, 23.

This righteousness is a gift from God. And even more astounding is the fact that the moment a sinner accepts Jesus, his status is immediately changed even before the person himself is changed! By that I mean that God declares us to be justified, or righteous, before our characters are changed. God accepts us as His sons and daughters even before we act like sons and daughters. The paralytic was justified before he was healed. Jesus accepted him as a son and called him a son while he was still in his awful condition.

This truth is at the very heart of the gospel, and it is one that Satan wants to keep hidden for obvious reasons, as we will discuss later. But settle it forever: your acceptance by God, your being called the son or daughter of God, is based upon the merits of Christ alone. All the good that you ever perform will never qualify you as His son or daughter. Nor do Christ's merits *complement* your own. We have no merits of our own to add to Christ's merits in any case. He is our righteousness before God. Thus, justification brings the *assurance* of salvation. It brings the *certainty* of our acceptance with God. It is *God's* achievement, not ours. There is no other way to have the peace of God in our hearts.

But the moment the sinner realizes that his guilt is transferred to the innocent, blameless, holy Son of God and that as an undeserving, repentant believer he is clothed with the righteousness of Christ, something happens inside him. This is why, as we shall see, justification implies more than a bit of legal fiction.

Satan and his agent, the beast, have attempted to thwart the everlasting gospel of salvation in Christ by substituting a counterfeit gospel—one in which salvation is achieved apart from God. This independence always involves disobedience to God—either by following one's own wishes in the place of God's will or by presuming so upon the merits of Christ that salvation seems assured regardless of obedience. Either extreme is a fake gospel and will result in receiving the mark of the beast as described in the warning of the third angel.

The

Warning Against

Counterfeits

And another angel, a third, followed them, saying with a loud voice, 'If any one worships the beast and its image, and receives a mark on his forehead or on his hand, he also shall drink the wine of God's wrath, poured unmixed into the cup of his anger, and he shall be tormented with fire and sulphur in the presence of the holy angels and in the presence of the Lamb. And the smoke of their torment goes up for ever and ever; and they have no rest, day or night, these worshipers of the beast and its image, and whoever receives the mark of its name.' Here is a call for the endurance of the saints, those who keep the commandments of God and the faith of Jesus" (Rev. 14:9-12, R.S.V.).

In these few words God has given mankind the most solemn, urgent warning that we can find anywhere in His Word. It constitutes the most vehement and fearful condemnation found in Scripture.

Have you ever had the nagging suspicion that God might actually enjoy seeing sinners receive what they deserve? The motorist who has had another car rocket past him can hardly conceal his satisfaction when, five miles down the highway, he sees the same automobile sitting bathed in the revolving light of a police car while its owner receives his richly deserved ticket. Everyone is pleased when the conceited bully finally takes on someone who can whittle him down to size! Does God feel the same way?

No, He does not! God *loves* sinners, no matter how obnoxious they may be. He loves them, no matter what they have done. He loves *you*, despite your sins and neglect of His love. And even though He cannot excuse sin, it hurts Him to see unrepentant sinners punished.

"As I live, saith the Lord God, I have no pleasure in the death of the wicked; but that the wicked turn from his way and live: turn ye, turn ye from your evil ways; for why will ye die?" (Eze. 33:11).

It is God's undying love for sinners that made Calvary possible. It is the same undying love that prompts Him to give sinful people warning after warning and appeal after appeal to turn from evil and accept forgiveness through faith in His Son Jesus Christ.

Don't misunderstand. God *will* punish sin unsparingly. And sinners who refuse to separate themselves from sin will be destroyed along with their sin. But God does not enjoy it. In fact, the Bible refers to His punishing of sinners as His "strange act" (Isa. 28:21). It is completely foreign to God's loving nature to destroy anything. That is why He showed the apostle John a vision of three angels flying through the sky announcing His final warning and appeal to the human race. In preceding chapters we have examined the first two of these angels and their messages. The third has the most fearful warning against sin to be found anywhere in the Bible—the warning against worshiping the beast or accepting its mark.

We have seen in previous chapters that the beast, as well as its image and mark, represents a worldwide antichrist system opposed to God and all that He stands for. It has as its focal point a false system of worship and a salvation that is a counterfeit to God's salvation by faith. In the setting of these messages, which go to the world in the last days before the return of Jesus, these two opposing systems—God's and Satan's—represent the final phase of the bitter controversy that has raged since sin began.

It is true that the battle has been fought since the very beginning, but Revelation 13 and 14 picture an intensification of the issues between Christ and Satan in the end of time just before Jesus comes again. The beast demands the homage and worship of the *entire world* (see Rev. 13:8, 14-17), and all except the relatively few who are faithful to the Lord Jesus Christ, will do so. Immediately following the three angels' messages, we read, "And behold a white cloud, and upon the cloud one sat like unto the Son of man, having on his head a golden crown, and in his hand a sharp sickle. And another angel came out of the temple, crying with a loud voice to him that sat on the cloud, Thrust in thy sickle, and reap: for the time is come for thee to reap; for the harvest of the earth is ripe. And he that sat on the cloud thrust in his sickle on the earth; and the earth was reaped" (Rev. 14:14-16).

Thus the attempt by the beast to impose its mark on men and women is the final issue in the great controversy between Christ and Satan.

Central to the life-and-death struggle over the true gospel is the valid relationship of law and grace (see Rev. 14:12). As we saw in a previous chapter dealing with the second angel's message of the fall of Babylon, this antichrist system, from a New Testament standpoint, applies first of all to Satan and in a subsidiary sense to his agents. First there was pagan Rome, then the medieval corruption of the Christian faith and its persecution by a state-church system, and in the last days a revival of this persecution by a world-encompassing confederacy of religious, political, and economic forces. This conglomerate will pose a threat to the very existence of God's faithful remnant who steadfastly worship Him according to His commandments.

In light of these thoughts, note that the blasphemous antichrist system so vividly described in Revelation 13:1-10 is not necessarily an avowed atheistic power. Atheism, by its very nature, is part of this worldwide system opposed to God, but the worst blasphemy is not that of an atheist who shakes his fist in God's face. Far more reprehensible and insidious (and therefore more dangerous) is the professed Christian who, despite his outward appearance, is a stranger to the actual character of Christ and who allows himself to be used as Satan's agent within the church itself. The rebuke of Christ to the Laodicean church (Rev. 3:14-22), which is symbolic of the condition of His followers in these last days, is significant: "I know thy works, that thou art neither cold nor hot: I would thou wert cold or hot. So then because thou art lukewarm, and neither cold nor hot, I will spue thee out of my mouth" (verses 15, 16).

The open rebellion of the avowed non-Christian is far less of a threat to Christ and His church than the lukewarm professed Christian who worships God only on his own terms. Thus the word *lukewarm* describes far more than sitting in the pew only at Christmas and Easter, accompanied by spasmodic financial support. Lukewarmness also includes failure to ascertain God's will through carelessness in study of the Scriptures; parroting of error because the majority would have it so; loyalty to a religious system merely because of family traditions; rationalizing disobedience to specific commands of God for the sake of unity and peace; acceptance of false principles in order to satisfy self-indulgent desires; and attempting to control men's minds through illicit use of religion.

Numerous examples of these and other blasphemous characteristics of lukewarmness are to be found in history and current events. The point is that blasphemy in one of its ugliest manifestations rears its head within the church itself in the form of those who claim God's name but who reject His authority over their lives. These may appear to be worshipers of God, but in essence they worship other gods—even the beast and its image.

Too often when we read Jesus' parable of the home built on foundations of sand (Matt. 7:24-27), we forget the preamble to that parable as well as its point. The introduction (verses 21-23) reveals that not all professed Christians will enter the kingdom. The Saviour is not here speaking to atheists or to a non-Christian society, but to those who have prophesied, cast out devils, and performed many wonderful things—all in the name of Jesus. Why is it that many of these will hear the words "Depart from me, ye that work iniquity"? The answer is plain. They have failed to conform their lives to God's will and to operate on the principles of His kingdom. They have created their own religious system and labeled it Christianity.

Revelation 14:12 indicates that obedience is the foundation of true worship. Notice a very important distinction here. Obedience is *not* the basis or foundation of salvation. Salvation is a free gift of God's grace apart from man's works. It is received by faith in Jesus Christ and His merits. (It is the beast's counterfeit gospel that puts works as the source of salvation.) But although obedience is not the foundation of salvation, it *is* the foundation of worship. When an individual has experienced God's saving grace, he or she will demonstrate that fact by loyal obedience as the foundation of worship. We cannot worship God while continuing in willful disobedience of His will! Anything less than obedience is iniquity. What could be more blasphemous than a self-proclaimed Christian who is actually working at cross purposes to God?

Returning to the parable, we find two homes on two different foundations—sand and stone. Note that the common denominator is that both builders erect homes; both builders are aware of how to build safely and correctly. The variable is that one obediently builds on bedrock according to the instructions of the

Master Designer, while the other contemptuously, blasphemously, builds in his own way on unsure sand. Here again we see the element of true worship versus false worship.

Obviously the rock foundation represents Christ. To build on Him means to base our lives on Him. This parable may be studied in conjunction with the prophet Isaiah's words to give a more complete picture: "Therefore thus saith the Lord God, Behold, I lay in Zion for a foundation a stone, a tried stone, a precious corner stone, a sure foundation: he that believeth shall not make haste" (Isa. 28:16).

All true worship is based on loyalty to God's commands, and nothing can take the place of absolute obedience to His will. King Saul at Gilgal appeared to be quite conscientious as he stood before Israel's army and offered a sacrifice to God, but his piety was hypocritical (see 1 Sam. 15). The king of Israel performed a religious worship service in direct opposition to the explicit command of God! This was not the first time Saul had set aside God's commands to follow the way that seemed right to him. Like many today, Saul was accustomed to making decisions on the basis of political expediency or economic considerations rather than on the basis of strict fidelity to God. God gave Saul his final opportunity to demonstrate loyalty to Him by commanding him to utterly destroy the Amalekites, including their livestock.

Despite God's careful instructions, Saul presumptuously followed his own inclinations. On his way home from the most brilliant victory that he had ever gained, Saul met the prophet Samuel, who had been sent to him by God. Debased by his disobedience, Saul greeted Samuel with lying lips: "Blessed be thou of the Lord: I have performed the commandment of the Lord. And Samuel said, What meaneth then this bleating of the sheep in mine ears, and the lowing of the oxen which I hear?" (1 Sam. 15:13, 14).

Saul began to excuse his disobedience by explaining that he had spared the best animals for sacrifices to God. When Samuel began to relate God's message of rebuke, Saul defiantly protested that he *had* done God's will. Samuel replied, "Hath the Lord as great delight in burnt offerings and sacrifices, as in obeying the voice of the Lord? Behold, to obey is better than sacrifice, and to hearken than the fat of rams. For rebellion is as the sin of witchcraft, and stubbornness is as iniquity and idolatry. Because thou hast rejected the word of the Lord, he hath also rejected thee from being king" (verses 22, 23).

This story perhaps describes best the issues at stake in the conflict between Satan and Christ as carried out by their followers—the beast worshipers of Revelation 13 and God's remnant of Revelation 14:12 "that keep the commandments of God, and the faith of Jesus." This latter group build on Christ the true foundation, not on some man-made sand foundation that cannot stand the test. Those who build on Him learn that worshiping the true God requires careful obedience to His building instructions.

It needs to be kept ever in mind that the only truly important thing in life is our eternal salvation. "What shall it profit a man, if he shall gain the whole world, and lose his own soul? Or what shall a man give in exchange for his soul?" (Mark 8:36, 37). The incomparable value of our salvation is best seen in the cost of the cross. In the light of the pricelessness of salvation, any attempt to change, ignore, or reject God's plan to save man is *blasphemy!* Any attempt to divert men's minds from Christ to an organization, a theory, or a person is *blasphemy.* Any substitution or counterfeit for the true gospel is *blasphemy.*

The Lord's ultimate concern for humanity is salvation—nothing more, nothing less, and nothing else. The ultimate concern of the prince of evil is to destroy humanity, and his most insidious way of destruction is to entice man with a counterfeit gospel. No wonder Jesus describes Satan as a murderer and such a liar that there is no truth in him (see John 8:44; 10:10). The beast described in Revelation 13:2 and warned against in chapter 14:9-12, receives his power, throne, and great authority from Satan the dragon (see chap. 12:9), and thus has similar characteristics. It is this beast, this antichrist conglomerate, that is the object of the most fearful threatenings God has ever addressed to mortals: "If any man worship the beast and his image, and receive his mark in his forehead, or in his hand, the same shall drink of the wine of the wrath of God, which is poured out without mixture into the cup of his indignation" (chap. 14:9, 10). Only those whose names are in the Lamb's book of life will be spared (see chap. 13:8).

What is the basic difference between those who worship the beast and his image and those who worship the Lamb, Christ Jesus? It is the same difference found between those who build on the Rock and those who build on the sand. As previously noted, that difference is found in two methods of salvation that can be traced from Genesis to Revelation. One is salvation by man's own methods and works, the other is salvation through grace by faith in Jesus Christ.

Now we come to an extremely important point. The elementary principle that supports the doctrine of salvation by faith is *God's creative power*. Man was made in God's image, but the power to produce life, to create life where there was none before, is uniquely God's. In His capacity to create life, God stands distinctly apart from any of His creatures. It is true that He has given a man and a woman the ability to produce a new life, but in so doing they are merely His agents. They simply pass on the life that He has already given to them. Man may procreate, reason, develop, invent, and accomplish amazing feats, but these are all only shadows of God's unique creative ability. Man can split an atom, but he can't make one! To command into existence something from nothing is one ability that God has never shared; He has reserved this power exclusively for Himself.

Not only is man unable to create life from nothing, he is unable to understand or discover the formula God used in doing so. For man to explain how God produced a single-celled amoeba would be a thousand times more difficult than it would be for an ant to solve the secrets of interplanetary space travel. All man can do (and it pleases God for man to do this) is to accept by faith God's creative power and ability. The tragedy is that many, especially in our modern age, are unwilling to do so. Instead of accepting God as Creator, they postulate theories of evolutionary development over vast ages of time, completely removing any need for an omnipotent Creator. Thus man becomes, once again, the arbiter of his own destiny, the one who decides his fate and manages his own affairs independently of God. This salvation (whatever form it may take) by man's own efforts and ingenuity is at the very root of the mark-of-the-beast principle of a counterfeit gospel. It is the age-old principle of sin—the independence of man from God.

I believe that the greatest single reason for our world's present chaotic condition is that man has failed to sense his responsibility and dependence on God. And in modern times this attitude is embodied most cogently in the evolutionary theory. After all, if man exists on earth as the result of an inexplicable process of accidental events—that is, if he just happened—then life really doesn't have ultimate meaning. It is, as Shakespeare expressed it, "a tale told by an idiot, full of sound and fury, signifying nothing." If such a world view is correct, is it any wonder that freakish violence is becoming increasingly commonplace, that survival by fair means or foul (whether in business or on the freeway or in politics) has become the name of the game? Is it any wonder that conventional standards of morality and decency are flouted openly? Why not, if there is no rational foundation for value judgments?

The doctrine of Creation is the foundation principle that gives meaning to life, both spiritual and physical. It is the foundation stone upon which all else is built. Note carefully the first chapter of Genesis, where the creative activity of God is emphasized. There is no hint of any evolutionary processes. There is no allusion to any elements of the heavens or the earth that came into existence by accident and continue to evolve by some unknown, unsponsored means. How significant that the opening chapters of the Bible picture *God* taking action. It is *God* who is creating. He wanted man never to lose sight of that important principle.

It seems significant to me that the same chapters of Genesis that bring so clearly to light God's creative activity in producing man also speak of the seventh-day Sabbath as a sacred day commemorating His creative power. Centuries later God saw fit to remind man of this important connection. In the heart of His ten-commandment law He instructed the human race to observe that day as holy, "for in six days the Lord made heaven and earth, the sea, and all that in them is, and rested the seventh day: wherefore the Lord blessed the sabbath day, and hallowed it" (Ex. 20:11).

Is it a coincidence that the society that has so largely turned from God as the Creator of heaven and earth has also largely forgotten the day He ordained to fasten their attention weekly to His creative power? I think not.

It is for this very reason that God is presented in the context of the three angels' messages as the Creator God. The first angel says, "Worship him that made heaven, and earth, and the sea, and the fountains of waters" (Rev. 14:7). In fact, as one reads through the Scriptures, he will note that the significant difference between the true God and all the false gods is His creative power. The argument for God's supremacy is consistently based upon His creatorship. "To whom then will ye liken me, or shall I be equal? saith the Holy One. Lift up your eyes on high, and behold who hath created these things" (Isa. 40:25, 26).

God is the source not only of man's physical existence but of his spiritual life as well. To restore the image of God in man through the new-birth experience is a work of creation. The apostle Paul recognized that David's words, "Create in me a clean heart, O God" (Ps. 51:10), were more than mere poetry. Paul himself echoed David's thought in 2 Corinthians 5:17 (R.S.V.): "If any one is in Christ, he is a new creation." This is a work that no finite man can do. Only the God who formed man of the dust of the ground and breathed into his nostrils the breath of life, can say, "I will take away the stony heart out of your flesh, and I will give you an heart of flesh" (Eze. 36:26).

The Bible opens with the proclamation of God's creatorship of the earth and all things in it. The predictive words of Revelation 14:7 give evidence likewise that in the final days of earth a sweeping announcement will go forth "to every nation, and kindred, and tongue, and people" (verse 6) to "worship him that made heaven, and earth, and the sea, and the fountains of waters."

The rejection of the Biblical Creation story undermines the central fact of the necessity of salvation by faith in Jesus Christ. Dr. Dan Gilbert used to tell audiences about the atheist's club he joined while in college. Its motto was: "Sons of apes don't need a Saviour." That's true. There is no basic compatibility between evolution, which assumes that we are pulling ourselves up by our own bootstraps, getting better and better, and the Bible assertion that man, created in the image of God, is now engaged in a senseless rebellion against his Maker and has no means of salvation in himself.

Now consider this important fact: Satan has intentionally attempted to blot out the truth of God's creative power from the minds of men. In fact, this refusal to accept God as his Creator was actually what led to Satan's downfall. Had Lucifer, as Satan was known before his sin, humbly admitted the creatorship of God, the fateful story of sin and the fall of man would never have been written.

Satan has blotted this truth from his own mind. He was forced to do so if his rebellion was ever to succeed. Satan denied God's creative and sustaining power. Notice that Lucifer's trouble began, not outwardly, but inwardly. This has been true of every single sin since then. Sin begins in the heart or the mind. According to Isaiah, Lucifer's problem was one of jealousy against God. "I will ascend . . . , I will exalt . . . : I will sit . . . : I will be like the most High" (Isa. 14:13, 14). These four "I's" of self-exaltation reveal the basic ingredient of sin—pride. Pride of self, pride of power, pride of position and ability—pride is the motto of the natural human heart.

Lucifer desired God's power, not His character; God's leadership, not His love; God's kingship, not His kindness; God's creative ability, not His goodness; God's honor, not His humility; God's position, not His personality. It was precisely at this point that the term *rebellion* was coined. What did it involve? It involved the setting up of a government complete with its own set of laws in opposition to God's government and laws. To counterfeit every phase of God's kingdom was Satan's aim. The very essence of Satan's kingdom is, "I can live by my own power." Thus began the mark-of-the-beast principle right in the very courts of heaven itself! It is a usurping of God's prerogatives and power. Those who will eventually be marked with the insignia of the beast will scream out, "I am my own authority; I am my own God."

It is interesting in this connection to note that scientists some years ago carefully tabulated the number of times mentally ill people used the words, "I," "me," "mine," "my," et cetera. These unfortunate people used such words referring to self at a rate of once in every twelve words of conversation. These same scientists recorded the speech of "normal" people and found such self-related words being used only once in every thirty-six words. In other words, the mentally unbalanced referred to self *three times more often* than those who were normal.

Did you notice the little phrase in the heart of the third angel's message: "They have no rest day nor night, who worship the beast and his image, and whosoever receiveth the mark of his name" (Rev. 14:11)? No doubt this refers primarily to the punishment such individuals will receive at the final judgment, but is it not also true that the wicked today have no rest day nor night? The most unpeaceful, unrestful human being in the world is one who walks about with a violated conscience and with no way to quiet it because he has turned away from the only Saviour.

Isaiah says, "There is no peace . . . unto the wicked" (chap. 48:22).

But those who operate on the seal-of-God principle and obey Him have a peace that cannot be explained and that cannot be destroyed. Those who accept the seal-of-God principle of salvation by faith in Jesus Christ are those who have "the patience of the saints" (Rev. 14:12). There is a quiet patience and confidence, an imperturbability about those who live by faith. These are the ones who continuously believe and operate on the principle that life and righteousness are theirs only by the gracious gift of God. Again, Isaiah says, "O that thou hadst hearkened to my commandments! then had thy peace been as a river, and thy righteousness as the waves of the sea" (chap. 48:18).

Thus we see in these messages of the three angels the battleground of the ages. The opposing forces are drawn up for a final conflict. On the one side is the crowd of rebellious created beings who have for their theme song, "I am my own God." These are the ones who will drink the wine of the wrath of God unmixed with mercy—not because He delights in punishing them, but because sin and sinners can have no place in a perfect universe. Theirs is an eternal death.

On the other side are a host of submissive, loving subjects of the true God who declare, "The Lord, He is God, and we are His children." In their midst is the cross of Christ, a symbol of the crucifixion of self. They have followed Isaiah's admonition, "Look unto me, and be ye saved, all the ends of the earth: for I am God, and there is none else" (chap. 45:22).

Thus the whole issue between Christ and Satan, between the marked ones and the sealed ones, centers on faith in Jesus Christ and a love for Him that automatically results in obedience to His will. The three angels' messages revolve about a single pillar: "For me to live is Christ" (Phil. 1:21). Only those who have this kind of relationship with our Lord, the lovely Jesus, will stand on the sea of glass having gotten the victory over the beast and its image and its mark (see Rev. 15:2).

There is only one way of achieving that victory— through faith in the Lord Jesus Christ. As we take up the concept of what is actually involved in exercising faith in Jesus, I beg you, as did the author of Hebrews, "consider . . . Jesus" (Heb. 3:1).

All
by Faith

Salvation, like an automobile, may be composed of various parts, but it must come in a package if it is to have any meaning or function at all. Remove the engine, or clutch, or spark plugs, or fuel pump from a car, and you really don't have a car. It may look like a car, but it can't function as a car. So it is with salvation. Remove or ignore any part of God's plan to save man and you may have people going about who look like Christians, who even claim to be Christians, but they do not function as Christians.

In the previous chapter we considered briefly the primary basis for salvation—justification. Although justification does not depend on our works; although it is what God does for the sinner; although it is not a mingling of God's works with our works; although it changes our status with God; although it is God's verdict, not our achievement; although it is the basis of our assurance and acceptance with God; although it includes pardon and forgiveness for our past sins; yet justification is never given to us as a gift all by itself. God's love is greater than that. The core of the salvation gift is justification, but along with it comes a change, a new-birth experience, and that involves a lifelong walk designated in the Scriptures as sanctification.

Justification settles our present account, but it also applies to our future as a covering umbrella from the moment we accept Christ until we meet the Lord. To omit sanctification from the plan of salvation and to focus only on justification is like a salesman trying to sell a car without brakes or steering mechanism. When God saves a person, not only does He do something *for* him, but He also does something *in* him.

At times ministers of various persuasions, on radio or television, in books and articles, narrowly define the gospel as the "doing and dying of Christ," separate from other important phases of salvation. This extreme position has led many to disregard the rules of God's kingdom contained in His holy law. It has led to an unbalanced belief in being saved without being changed, and it deprives a person of the full benefits of God's glorious plan to save man. Suppose the loving parents of a crippled child learn that a delicate surgical process will correct the problem. Will they not make any sacrifice to enable their little one to function normally? What a horrible injustice to allow a youngster to suffer a physical handicap when it could be eliminated!

What kind of a God would our heavenly Father be if in His salvation plan He performs something *for* men but does nothing *in* man? When the Holy Spirit draws a person to Christ, the primary burden is guilt and the primary joy is the joy of forgiveness. Nothing quite equals this experience. But following a close second is the burden of sinful inclinations and desires and the joy of overcoming them. Now, if God forgives and justifies a man but leaves him to wallow in the mire of lust, violent temper, pride, selfishness, and immorality, would He not be denying His own character of love and perfection? God's love forbids Him to allow His children to live in a crippled condition when He can correct our handicaps. And He will if we permit Him. We must understand that God is not in the business of building living memorials to mediocrity! Rather God is in the re-creating business—the business of making men over new (see 2 Cor. 5:21).

The Greek work for *gospel* is similar to our English word *evangelize*. It means to tell the good news, to announce the glad tidings. What is the good news? What are the glad tidings? It is the wonderful truth that Jesus the Son of God entered our planet as a baby, walked among men as a man, taught, healed, changed the lives of men, suffered, died, was resurrected, and now continues this same work in heaven as our High Priest. He is *now* forgiving sins, dispensing His healing benefits as High Priest to all those who allow themselves to be drawn to Him through His Holy Spirit. So the gospel, like an automobile, is a marvelous package, which when received not only changes our standing with God but changes also our attitudes and actions toward God and our fellow men.

Some may wish to distinguish between the gospel and the change brought about by receiving the gospel, calling this change the *fruitage* of the gospel. Such distinctions may be fine from a theoretical view, but the important point is that in our experience we can never separate what God does *for* us from what God does *in* us! They go together like a door and its hinges. Justification, the door, is not the hinges. Sanctification, the hinges, is not the door. But both are part of the gospel "home." Anything less than this becomes a false system of salvation and part of the mark-of-the-beast system. Satan is just as pleased when individuals think that eternal life can be theirs without a new-birth experience as he is over those who are working night and day to buy eternal life with the money of works! Either extreme is equally false and equally disastrous.

May I add one more point from my own personal experience? I am constantly aware of my faults, shortcomings, weaknesses, mistakes, and sins. How depressed and discouraged I would be if I believed that my assurance of salvation depended upon my performance. Despair would overwhelm me, and in the past, before I had a deeper understanding of how God saves, it has overwhelmed me. Yet at the same time, while I no longer look to myself for assurance of salvation, I am also aware of my responsibility to God. "Responsibility" involves the idea of responding to any given situation. In the case of salvation, my "response" to what Christ has done *for* me is to permit Him to do something *in* me. When I say "permit," I mean I am eager—in fact have an unutterable longing—for God to change me inside. Thus, I am very much aware of the change that God has made, and is making, in me.

Every Christian should have this experience. Paul certainly knew something happened *in* him (as well as *to* him) on the road to Damascus. He fell to the ground as a lost sinner (his name then was Saul), and although temporarily blinded by light from heaven, rose to his feet as a born-again man! (Please read his thrilling conversion story in Acts 9:1-22.) Paul became a mighty weapon in God's hand and lived a sanctified life. Yet in his later years, shortly before his martyrdom, he wrote a letter to a young man named Timothy in which he said, "Christ Jesus came into the world to save sinners; of whom I am chief" (1 Tim. 1:15). Paul did not say, "I was first and foremost of sinners," but "I *am.*" In Ephesians 3:8 the same man declared himself to be "less than the least of all saints." This was no mock humility on the great apostle's part, but rather a true expression of his feelings—feelings that are shared by every true Christian.

The experience I have just described of a person who becomes a Christian is a paradox. It is an experience that is almost impossible to put into writing. For instance, the more I look to Jesus and understand what He has done, and is doing, to save me, the more I become like Him. And the more I become like Jesus, the more I see my own sinfulness and feel my own unworthiness. The more I advance in the Christian life through the process of sanctification, the more I am aware of the need to advance. Thus, paradoxically, the gulf between my profession and performance seems to be ever widening as my acquaintance with my Saviour deepens. But there are at least two reasons why I don't give up in this potentially discouraging situation. First, above all else, I know that my salvation depends on Christ alone, not on myself. When my Lord returns and I hear the words "Well done," do you think for a moment I will ever feel that I *deserve* to hear those words? Do you think that those words will make me feel that I have a *right* to enter His eternal kingdom? Never! Throughout eternity I will never, never cease to praise *Him* for His salvation. The only reason I will ever be in heaven is Jesus. My works will never get me there—never!

The second reason I am not discouraged is because I am aware that although my defects are painfully evident, God *has* given me a new heart, and by His grace I *am* progressing in the Christian life, even though it be ever so slowly. Thus there is an inward confirmation that I am growing, slow as it is, in the right direction. In my experience, I call justification the assurance factor and sanctification the confirmation factor.

Now let me come to another point that needs careful consideration. Is our obedience to God's will (as some assert) composed partly of our efforts and partly of God's? No! Such is not the case! God must have the total credit for all phases of salvation—past, present, and future.

"But we must cooperate with God in the sanctification process," some insist. Of course sanctification requires our cooperation, but it also requires our cooperation to be justified—and that cooperation is called believing. To believe and accept by faith that God justifies me is really no different than believing and accepting by faith that God sanctifies me. This is a key point in understanding victory over sin. I have never been able in my own experience to distinguish between the quality of faith that accepts God's gift of justification and the quality of faith that accepts God's gift of sanctification. It requires an enormous amount of the gift of faith to believe that God justifies me and declares me righteous when my faulty emotions madly struggle to tell me that I have to do something or give something to earn God's favor. Those same emotions also scream at me that God can't call me righteous when I am so wicked! But faith, and faith alone, must rise above these feelings to lay hold of the magnificent truth that God does justify me, by faith alone, through the grace of Jesus Christ.

Likewise, it also requires an enormous amount of the gift of faith to believe daily that God can and will give me victory over every wrong action—even wrong thoughts! There is always the emotional tendency to feel that I can overcome anything by trying hard enough or at least by trusting a combination of His help and my effort. There is also a tendency at times to believe that I am what I am and that I can't really change. God must take me as I am, if at all. But, with Paul, we must ever remember the question, "What do you have that you did not receive?" (1 Cor. 4:7, N.I.V.).

Salvation—both justification and sanctification—is all of God. Did we create ourselves? Even the ability to think—an action of the brain—is a gift from God. The consequence of justification is sanctification, but both are received and experienced by faith in Christ alone.

God is not interested merely in *justifying* us; He wants to *change* us. A parent may forgive an erring

130

child but the ultimate goal and hope of the parent is to see a change in the child, both for his own happiness and also for the parent's joy. The story of the prodigal son ended in happiness and joy because he returned in submission to his father's will. But the desire and strength to return was given to him as a gift from God. The prodigal son's only part in the returning process was to believe that his father would accept him, not on the basis of his own performance even in returning home but on the basis of the father's love. What a tragedy if the story had ended with the prodigal son's deciding that because of his decision to come home and the effort he made in returning he deserved to be received and welcomed and forgiven!

The angel announced to Joseph that Mary would give birth to a son whose name would be Jesus "because he will save his people *from* their sins" (Matt. 1:21, N.I.V., emphasis supplied), not save His people *in* their sins.

To believe that sanctification is a combination of our effort and God's grace, while justification is by faith alone, leads inevitably to the despicable state of pride. If we see sanctification as partly a result of *our* effort, every evidence of growth in Christ becomes a cause for taking credit to ourselves. We may outwardly seem to be advancing, but inwardly we are going backward. It is the age-old struggle between righteousness by works and righteousness by faith. It is the age-old struggle between what I can do and what God can do. It is the age-old struggle between taking credit to self and giving God the credit for everything.

The apostle Paul assures us that "it is God which

worketh in you both to will and to do of his good pleasure" (Phil. 2:13). The theme song of every individual who finally stands before God in eternity will be that of the twenty-four elders of Revelation who "fall down before him that sat on the throne, and worship him that liveth for ever and ever, and cast their crowns before the throne, saying, Thou art worthy, O Lord, to receive glory and honour and power: for thou hast created all things, and for thy pleasure they are and were created." "For thou wast slain, and hast redeemed us to God by thy blood out of every kindred, and tongue, and people and nation" (Rev. 4:10, 11; 5:9).

How great our Lord is!

The
Comprehensive
Ten

When my brother-in-law, an employee of the Newport News (Virginia) Shipbuilding Company, took me on a tour of the facilities right after World War II ended, one ship, the S.S. *America*, caught my attention. Its story has special meaning to the Christian.

Our country's largest and most luxurious passenger liner at the time, the vessel had previously been turned over to the Government for transporting troops to Europe. The Government instructed the Newport News Shipbuilding Company, the original builders, to store carefully every rug, mirror, piece of furniture, and anything else not needed for its actual operation. Workmen replaced the lovely decorations and appointments with military bunks, enabling the ship to carry ten times more soldiers than it had tourist passengers. After the war, the Government contracted with the same company to restore the ship to its original condition.

As I accompanied my brother-in-law through the dry-docked ship, I saw workers unwrapping tables, pictures, couches, and chairs and replacing them in newly redecorated salons, cabins, and dining rooms.

Every detail of the restoration had been precisely cared for, using the original architectural plans for the ship. Nothing, minute or extensive, was overlooked. When it was all done, a special relaunching of the S.S. *America* was scheduled. At the appropriate moment the gleaming, totally renovated ship slipped back into the water and again became the pride of America's passenger liners. A fantastic job had been done in converting the mighty ocean vessel.

In the beginning God created a gorgeous planet. Possibly it was the most luxurious one He had ever brought into existence. He fashioned a pair of beings in His own image, placed them in their brand-new world, and instructed them to care for it and fill it with beings who, like themselves, would be loving and obedient subjects of their Creator. His instructions, or "architectural plans," were carefully conveyed to our first parents. But a terrible thing happened. War came. The enemy of God carried his rebellion of sin to God's new world. This planet and its first occupants became involved, and what was once a perfect, beautiful place inhabited by two holy creatures turned into a murderous battleground. Everything, including Adam and Eve, was now under sin's curse. Even the atmosphere became subject to great changes hitherto unknown. Leaves fell; flowers drooped; thorns and thistles appeared. Man's nature changed so rapidly that murder took place in the very next generation! The earth and its inhabitants have suffered terribly ever since.

But God introduced a salvaging plan immediately after sin occurred. This plan called for a total and perfect restoration of all that sin touched, and it was taught to man during Old Testament days by an elaborate system of services known as the sanctuary ritual. By means of symbols this system portrayed in detail God's plan to restore man from the effects of sin. We have discussed at length, in previous chapters, several of the important steps in this process. There are other steps we haven't had space to discuss in this limited volume. However, on page 157 you will find an advertisement for a free Bible study course by mail. Be sure to take advantage of this opportunity, for with the course you will receive, also free, a copy of the book *Steps to Christ*. This 96-page book has been a constant companion of mine. It has one of the largest circulations of any religious book in the world and has been translated into 103 languages. Literally millions of people, young and old, have been greatly blessed by it.

In the previous chapter we discussed the place of sanctification in God's plan for restoration. We need always to keep in mind that the grand objective of God's redemptive work is the restoration of man and our planet to the original, pre-sin condition. Like the job done on the S.S. *America*, total, complete, and perfect restoration is God's ultimte objective for us. You see, Christ not only redeems us from the *penalty* of sin (which is justification) but He redeems us from the *power* of sin (which is sanctification). When He returns the second time, He will deliver us from the *presence* of sin. In other words, Christ not only redeems us from sin, He redeems us for His Father and Himself!

To achieve this objective requires the bringing of man into conformity to Christ's will. What do we mean when we speak of "Christ's will"? We mean His holy moral law of ten commandments as found in Exodus 20:1-17. It is this law that God promises to write on our hearts. "I will put my laws into their mind, and write them in their hearts: and I will be to them a God, and they shall be to me a people" (Heb. 8:10). In this added explanation of the new-birth experience, notice carefully that it is *God* who puts His laws, His will, into our hearts. We are totally incapable of doing this of ourselves. Those operating on the mark-of-the-beast principle try in their own strength to satisfy God and His requirements, but God's way is much different.

It is an important point, too, that God gave Israel His law *after* He delivered the people from slavery. So it is with us. He writes His law in our hearts *after* we have been delivered from our guilty enslavement in spiritual bondage. The very introduction of the Ten Commandments brings out this point: "I am the Lord thy God, which have brought thee out of the land of Egypt, out of the house of bondage" (Ex. 20:2). Before He begins to command, God reminds the people that He has saved them. A knowledge of, and obedience to, the law must be preceded by a deliverance from the bondage of guilt, and by a new-birth experience. If this order is reversed, obedience becomes a work system and we slip immediately into the mark-of-the-beast syndrome. The law was never given as a means of earning salvation. Rather, the law is a standard that gives the converted person a knowledge of how to show his loyalty and gratitude to the One who has saved him and whom he loves above all else.

Some Christians, in an effort to avoid keeping certain commandments, use a statement of Jesus in an erroneous setting. Our Lord pointed out in Matthew 22:37-40 that the two great commandments on which the law and the prophets hang, are a total love for God and a love for our neighbor equal to the love we have for ourselves. In this way Jesus summarized the Ten Commandments: the first four demonstrate what is involved in loving God supremely; the last six spell out how to love our fellowman even as we love ourselves. The human mind is incapable of knowing specifically how to love God and our fellowman in such a total way. God must give us the details, and He has.

Please take your Bible and turn to Exodus 20. Beginning with verse 3, compare each of the Ten Commandments with the following comments: The first commandment (verse 3) very logically begins with God's supremacy, so that man will make no mistake about *who* he should worship. This commandment affirms to us that the universe is run by the harmonious intelligence of an all-wise, all-powerful God—not by happenstance or blind chance! Eliminate or disobey the first commandment, and atheism or evolution becomes man's god. The second, third, and fourth commandments (verses 4-11) reveal *how* we should and should not worship the true God. The fifth commandment (verse 12) is designed to help man maintain self-respect by honoring his parents. With this commandment we shift from those indicating love for God and take up those dealing with love for our fellowmen. Life is protected and made sacred by the sixth commandment (verse 13). The seventh (verse 14) protects the sacredness of the family circle. The eighth (verse 15) safeguards man's property; the ninth (verse 16) maintains man's confidence in the word of his neighbor and enables society to operate effectively. In the tenth commandment (verse 17) God probes deeply into the mind of man.

Some have called it the "law of the unenforcible." When God told His people not to covet, He was saying in effect, "You must be born again." While the first nine rules deal mainly with observable actions, the tenth is concerned with the state of man's mind.

Too many of us are like the covetous man in an old fable to whom Zeus promised anything he wanted on the condition that his neighbor should receive twice as much as himself. The envious fellow thought it over, and decided to ask for the loss of one eye!

These ten comprehensive laws cover, in principle, every situation and aspect of life. Nothing is omitted. We may sum them up as follows: the first, loyalty; the second, commitment; the third, reverence; the fourth, worship; the fifth, honor; the sixth, appreciation; the seventh, purity; the eighth, honesty; the ninth, truthfulness; and the tenth, unselfishness.

The great struggle between Christ and Satan—the struggle that is the focal point of the three angels' messages—is actually over the law of God. There is the real hub of the controversy, and all through human history the conflicts faced by Christians and followers of God have inevitably centered on the commands of God versus the commands of men. The most effective way to overthrow any government is to undermine its constitution. Satan knows this, and his attacks are consistently aimed at destroying the spirit, the letter, the principles, of God's law. Society today, apparently on the point of an almost complete breakdown of authority and decency, readily demonstrates how successful the enemy has been. There is not a single commandment of the ten that has not come under attack and that is not now being rebelled against and openly disregarded by many.

For example, the adulation and worship being given to the gods of intellectualism, science, wealth, materialism, and self violates the first commandment. Millions, in defiance of the second commandment, have erected all kinds of "idols" in their lives to take the place of God. Even professedly Christian churches are filled with literal images of saints, apostles, and others that are bowed to, caressed, kissed, and worshiped! The Lord's name is recklessly used by profane persons despite the third commandment. And, of course, those who claim to be Christians but who do not act as such are not guiltless, for they also misuse His name. The fourth commandment asks for us to remember to keep the Sabbath day holy. Such a widespread disregard for this command exists that we have reserved comment for the next chapter.

Those precepts that deal with our relationship to fellow human beings have fared no better than the first four. The honoring of parents has been largely forgotten by millions of children. Murder statistics indicate that the sixth commandment is being violated at an ever-increasing pace, but more than this, "murder" in the form of hatred and racial, political, and social prejudice seems to be the order of the day. The "new morality" has virtually destroyed the seventh commandment. In fact, purity and modesty are such "museum pieces" that our society ridicules anyone trying to uphold seriously this commandment. Theft (commandment eight) has reached such proportions that insurance rates skyrocket and other forms of dishonesty have kept pace. Falsification and lying are a way of life for many. Covetousness is no longer sin, but "in."

When one considers the near collapse of morality and the breakdown of all that is decent and realizes that this situation is worldwide in scope, it is truly frightening. Yet, in the midst of this chaotic rebellion, God has a people who are committed to Him. These, and those who unite with them, will show to the universe what God's grace can accomplish in an individual who surrenders to His control. God is bringing about transformations of life so amazing that Satan, with all his wisdom, stands baffled.

At the beginning of this book I mentioned God's last message to the world in the form of three angels' messages found in Revelation 14. A careful study of this chapter shows that there will be a remnant who, by God's grace, will be found blameless when Jesus returns. This group will not be a great multitude, but only a small number compared to the world's population. By trusting Jesus, however, they refuse submission to the beast's power. As a result they receive the seal of God, the seal of His approval. Their loyalty and obedience to Him clearly delineate them from the rebellious multitudes who have rejected the pleadings of the Holy Spirit.

The final verse of the third angel's message dealing with the mark of the beast makes the issue clear. "This calls for patient endurance on the part of the saints who obey God's commandments and remain faithful to Jesus" (Rev. 14:12, N.I.V.). This verse climaxes God's warning against the mark of the beast and puts in true perspective the relationship of law and gospel. It is not keeping the law in order to be saved, but it is obedience to God because of the Holy Spirit's sanctifying presence in the heart. Such obedience is God's seal; obedience from any other motive is really not obedience at all and is the mark of the beast.

Rest

for the

Restless

As I come to this final chapter I feel I have just touched with the finger tips, as it were, a few of the more important themes dealing with God's incomparable plan to save His children. One theme, previously mentioned, relates to the warning against receiving the mark of the beast: "There is no rest day or night for those who worship the beast and his image, or for anyone who receives the mark of his name" (Rev. 14:11, N.I.V.).

I have dealt with the problem of guilt and its solution through God's forgiveness, emphasizing the comparison between false systems of salvation and the only true way—the mark of the beast versus the seal of God. Peace, rest, love, and joy come only to those who accept God's method of restoration. Those who refuse the Lord's way literally have no rest day or night. They are driven by guilt, obsessed with sin. At best fearfulness, worry, and concern mark their days.

But the peace and rest the Lord offers is just as literal as the unrest the mark-of-the-beast system offers. Jesus stated it tenderly and beautifully in Matthew 11:28-30: "'Come to me, all you who are weary and burdened, and I will give you rest. Take my yoke upon you and learn from me, for I am gentle and humble in heart, and you will find rest for your souls. For my yoke is easy and my burden is light'" (N.I.V.). This passage sounds paradoxical. How can one find rest by taking a burden and a yoke? Before coming to Jesus we are laden and burdened with our own works and worldly cares. The worst burden of all is the heavy load of sin and guilt. But Jesus' burden and yoke—justification and sanctification—are rest and peace to the soul.

If people ever needed rest and peace, they do now! Even our poor earth, torn and tattered like an old garment by drought, fire, earthquake, flood, and volcanic eruption, needs rest. The animal kingdom, diseased, hunted, and slaughtered, needs peace and rest. Our world, with its resources depleted, its lakes, streams, oceans, and atmosphere polluted, is rapidly becoming a vast garbage heap. Oh, how it needs rest, peace, and restoration!

But the degradation that has come to our lovely planet, terrible as it is, is infinitesimal compared to what has happened to man. Often I have scanned the faces of people in crowded stores, subways, streets, buses, and airliners, asking myself, "What sorrow and hurt are those individuals experiencing?" My heart cries out, "Oh, if only they would permit the Holy Spirit to bring them to the One who can take their burden and give them rest!" Faces everywhere have stamped upon them guilt, greed, lust, anxiety, fear, timidness, sickness, discontent. So few portray peace and love. The enormous amount of pain, suffering, and loneliness is beyond statistical reports. The whole world groans in the grip of death. In the United States alone nearly 30,000 people a year hopelessly take their own lives, while 20,000 others who want to live are murdered. It is pointless to add more color to such a gruesome painting. News reports alone, with their tales of man's inhumanity to man, are sufficient to batter the mind into a state of insensitivity.

I have tried to share with you in this book what the Lord wants to do for us. Now I must expand one more point. God in Eden created a memorial of peace and rest for man to remember. This memorial ties together the themes of Creation, redemption, and final restoration. It is not a memorial of cement and steel; it is not a hallowed spot; it is a memorial of *time. Time* is a universal commodity, and no matter where man goes on earth, this memorial can ever be with him. This memorial is the seventh-day Sabbath. Let the Word speak for itself: "Thus the heavens and the earth were completed in all their vast array. By the seventh day God had finished the work he had been doing; so on the seventh day he rested from all his work. And God blessed the seventh day and made it holy, because on it he rested from all the work of creating that he had done" (Gen. 2:1-3, N.I.V.).

Adam and Eve were created on the sixth day of the week; their first full day of life was spent celebrating this twenty-four-hour memorial in time with their Creator-God. It was a celebration of human beginnings—the inauguration of all human history.

After man sinned, God placed in the heart of the Ten Commandments the Sabbath command. It is the only one of the ten that begins with the word *remember.* There was a definite reason for this. He never wanted man to forget his "roots," because whenever man forgets his origins he is possessed with restlessness.

The majority, even of Christians, ridicule the Genesis story of Creation, but I agree with Britain's great prime minister Sir Winston Churchill, who said, "We reject, however, with scorn all those learned and labored myths that Moses was but a legendary figure. . . . We believe that the most scientific view, the most up-to-date and rationalistic conception, will find its fullest satisfaction in taking the Bible story literally. . . . We may be sure that all these things happened just as they are set and according to Holy Writ."

Personally, I don't need Mr. Churchill's support for believing the Genesis record. I know by experience the joy and assurance that the Creation story, and its seventh-day Sabbath rest, has brought to my life. The Sabbath tells me that God is a perfect and loving Creator who has such infinite care for His creatures that He provides for all our human needs. God has not overlooked our frailties, and for our good and enjoyment He has commanded us to keep holy the seventh-day Sabbath. Thus the Sabbath, like a portable sanctuary, can be a blessing for man wherever he is on our round world, even behind prison bars.

Samuele Bacchiocchi, a personal friend, in his book *Divine Rest for Human Restlessness* has enumerated many beautiful things connected with the Sabbath, some of which I want to incorporate in this chapter. He points out that the true Sabbath rest is

145

intimately connected with the redemptive rest Jesus offers His followers. This rest of redemption is reflected in the book of Hebrews: "And God did rest the seventh day from all his works" (chap. 4:4). The author of Hebrews shows that the Genesis Sabbath rest foreshadowed a fuller realization that had dawned with the coming of Jesus. "There remains, then, a Sabbath-rest for the people of God" (verse 9, N.I.V.). Thus the seventh-day Sabbath is inseparably bound up with salvation through Jesus. It is by accepting *Him* as Lord and Saviour that we can at last enter into the rest that the gospel brings (see Heb. 4:10, 11). It is the good news of God's rest—release from the guilt and the power, and finally from the very presence, of sin—that is promised and memorialized by the seventh day of creation, the Sabbath memorial.

The implications of true seventh-day Sabbath observance are far-reaching. First and foremost, the Sabbath is established as a memorial of Creation and of *re*-creation (salvation—the new-birth experience). It is the answer to the evolutionary theory, which has destroyed man's true roots, and the fruitage of which has led to anarchy, immorality, disrespect, and all that goes with the rule of might and greed. When properly kept, the Sabbath lengthens life, increases productivity, and blesses one with better health. It is truly the Lord's day (see Matt. 12:8), and it is just as necessary for our happiness and contentment today as when originally made and given to man in Eden.

But above and beyond all, the Sabbath, in the light of the cross, is a time to celebrate both the good news of God's perfect creation and the good news of Christ's complete redemption. The Sabbath day is a time to remember His rest of forgiveness and salvation. In fact, to the understanding Christian, the Sabbath becomes a seal, a sign, of God's salvaging operation on the heart. No, it is not a seal or mark that human eyes can see, but God and His angels know who are His devoted, loyal, submissive, happy children. Those who by faith in their Saviour Jesus Christ obey all His commandments, including the fourth, or Sabbath, command, show they are God's special possession and give evidence that they are covered with Christ's righteousness. Didn't Jesus say, "If ye love me, keep my commandments" (John 14:15)? Those who observe the seventh-day Sabbath, in spite of possible ridicule and persecution, will surely be careful to observe the other nine commandments. The person who refuses to trample on God's holy time will certainly be careful in his treatment of the lives and property of others. The person who observes the seventh-day Sabbath will certainly be a true believer in all the Scriptures, including the Creation record. Such will certainly recognize the supremacy of God in their lives. Above all, the person who understands and keeps the seventh-day Sabbath will know that creation and salvation are *God's* works and not his own. He understands why God tells us, " 'Keep my Sabbaths holy, that they may be a sign between us. Then you will know that I am the Lord your God' " (Eze. 20:20, N.I.V.).

If you study carefully the fourth commandment, you will find in the Sabbath command the seal of God's whole commandment law. It is the only one that reveals the three important elements found on any government or king's seal his name, his title or authority, and the extent of his dominion. "For in six days the Lord made heaven and earth" (Ex. 20:11). His name is the Lord; His authority or title is Creator; and His dominion is heaven and earth. This commandment not only authenticates the whole law; it also authenticates and seals the person who by faith accepts Christ as his Saviour and Lord.

It is interesting to note that the Sabbath commandment is the only one of the ten that a person can openly violate and still be regarded by other people as a good Christian. But those who allow God to have full sway in their lives will obey Him—not to earn salvation, but because Christ is enthroned in their hearts. The Sabbath thus becomes the outward sign or seal of an inward experience. In these final hours of earth's history, God's last message as found in Revelation 14:6, 7 calls mankind to accept the everlasting gospel and to "worship him that made heaven, and earth, and the sea, and the fountains of waters." The worship of God as Creator and re-Creator is part of His final salvaging plan for man. This is the reason a worldwide message is penetrating every island, jungle, continent, and country through books, television, radio, and personal visits, inviting men and women to accept the everlasting gospel and to honor the Saviour by permitting His Spirit to lead them into an obedience that includes the observance of Saturday, the seventh-day Sabbath. Thus the Sabbath is becoming an outward symbol, or sign or seal, of God's faithful remnant who follow Jesus fully.

Before our Lord returns, He intends to show the universe that in spite of Satan's rebellion, individuals from every nation, tribe, language, and people can, through their committed Christian lives, experience salvation by faith alone in Jesus Christ—by faith alone be "born again, not of perishable seed, but of imperishable, through the living and enduring word of God" (1 Peter 1:23, N.I.V.).

In contrast to those who faithfully adhere to the seal-of-God principle, we find a host who follow the beast and worship him. This group includes almost the entire world (see Rev. 13:3). In fact, the beast system is so vast and influential that John declares, "All inhabitants of the earth will worship the beast—all whose names have not been recorded in the book of life belonging to the Lamb" (Rev. 13:8, N.I.V.). As pointed out before, this beast system operates on the principle of salvation by works. Man becomes his own God and operates independently of his Creator. He may claim to serve the true God and may even exhibit Christian qualities in his life, but self-supremacy is shown by the fact that when God's will cuts across his own desires, he adheres to his own standards, makes his own decisions, and believes what he wants to believe, without reference to what God says in the Scriptures. He even creates his own plans for salvation and his own rules by which to achieve it.

Therefore this multifaceted system includes as many plans, doctrines, and beliefs as there are people who follow them. The world is filled with all kinds of religions, but at the heart and core of them all, save one—true Christianity—is the do-it-yourself concept.

Most of Christianity itself, sad to say, operates on this principle.

It is apostate Christianity, however, that takes the lead in opposing those who remain faithful to God and His commandments. It is apostate Christianity that is foremost in urging upon the world the mark of the beast. Thus, in the days just prior to the coming of Jesus, the lines are clearly drawn. On the one hand are those who in loyalty to Jesus Christ, their Saviour, accept His seal of divine approval by accepting His righteousness and giving evidence of their love by their obedience to His commandments. On the other hand are those forces opposed to God's will—led by fallen Babylon, apostate Christianity. In disregard of God, these insist on following their own method of salvation independently of their Creator—the principle of salvation by works.

One can find every rule, standard, regulation, and doctrine imaginable even among Christians. The variances of belief and practice are numerous and wide. From baptism to Communion, from the Second Coming to the nature of mankind, from tithing to the millennium, Christians hold an unbelievable array of disparate beliefs. Logic alone tells us that they cannot *all* be correct. If the Scriptures teach us anything, they teach us that God is a God of order. God is not a part of Babylon, confusion. We have "one Lord, one faith, one baptism; one God and Father of all" (Eph. 4:5, 6, N.I.V.). "Small is the gate and narrow the road that leads to life, and only a few find it" (Matt. 7:14, N.I.V.). Not because God is difficult to find do few make their way to Him, but because the love of self, peer pressure, materialism, et cetera, build barriers between man and his God.

I must mention one common belief that is held and practiced by nearly the entire Christian world, and yet has absolutely *no* scriptural foundation. This will come as a shock to some, because the Christian world has so overwhelmingly accepted this unscriptural concept. Although it may be perplexing, I urge you to study thoughtfully and carefully what is truth. I am referring to the observance of the first day of the week, Sunday, as a holy day. Of course, only a tiny minority really honor Sunday, since for most Christians Sunday is a day not only for church but for everything from sports to automobile repairs. I am convinced that when we consider those who actually observe a day—be it Saturday, the seventh day, or Sunday, the first day—in the specific way God requires in the fourth commandment, there are more Christians who keep holy the seventh-day Sabbath than there are Christians who keep "holy" the first day, Sunday. On the first day of the week the attention is not exclusively given to the Lord. Nevertheless, Sunday still stands as a day of worship for the Christian world in general. The non-Christian world, too, recognizes it as a "Christian" day.

The doctrine of Sunday worship is the one belief on which more Christians agree than any other single doctrine. Sunday is the most visible, outwardly tangible symbol that identifies Christians in every nation on earth. Even in such non-Christian nations as Japan, more factories and stores are closed on Sunday than on any other day. Yet for this widely held, common belief there is no scriptural authority, no indication that it forms part of God's sanctifying will for those who have accepted His righteousness and salvation. Sunday observance stands in unique contrast to the seventh-day Sabbath of God, the outward sign of the seal of God.

Please understand that I do not believe that, of itself, Sabbathkeeping can save a person any more than can honoring one's parents. I am referring to the *results* of salvation in a person's life. Those results are seen in the willingness of one who has been saved to allow the Holy Spirit to bring his life daily into harmony with the commandments of God.

Notice carefully how the contrast is drawn between those who receive the beast's mark and those who do not. After describing the awful fate of those who accept the mark of the beast, John calls attention, by way of contrast, to those who remain faithful to God. He says, "Here is the patience [or endurance] of the saints: here are they that keep the commandments of God, and the faith of Jesus" (Rev. 14:12).

In other words, the issue is loyalty to God as exhibited by faithful obedience to His will, or commandments. Those who accept the seal of God's divine approval patiently, willingly, keep His commandments. Those who receive the mark of the beast disobey God in order to follow the dictates of the beast.

In fact, Satan's deceptions can be so subtle that many of those who honor the beast and receive his mark will do so thinking that they are honoring God. The apostle Paul, referring to this same beast power as "the lawless one," speaks of those who "perish because they refused to love the truth," and "for this reason God sends them a powerful delusion so they will believe the lie" (2 Thess. 2:10, 11, N.I.V.).

It is an amazing tribute to the cunning and skill of Satan that he has been able to persuade millions of Christians to disregard, either willfully or ignorantly, the one commandment God has given that points directly to Him as the Creator. It seems that Satan has concentrated his attack on this commandment because he knows how important it is in directing men and women to God as the Creator and re-Creator of their lives.

Listen to what God says: " 'Remember the sabbath day, to keep it holy. Six days you shall labor, and do all your work; but the seventh day is a sabbath to the Lord your God; in it you shall not do any work, you, or your son, or your daughter, your manservant, or your maidservant, or your cattle, or the sojourner who is within your gates; for in six days the Lord made heaven and earth, the sea, and all that is in them, and rested the seventh day; therefore the Lord blessed the sabbath day and hallowed it' " (Ex. 20:8-11, R.S.V.).

It almost seems that the angel had this commandment (the fourth of the Ten Commandments) in mind as he flew through the air calling out, "Worship him who made heaven and earth, the sea and the fountains of water" (Rev. 14:7, R.S.V.).

God Himself points to Creation as the meaning for the Sabbath commandment. By keeping the seventh day holy, His people show their loyalty to Him as Creator. The Bible record of Creation tells us: "Thus the heavens and the earth were finished, and all the host of them. And on the seventh day God finished his work which he had done, and he rested on the seventh day from all his work which he had done. So God blessed the seventh day and hallowed it" (Gen. 2:1-3, R.S.V.).

At the very beginning of our world God set aside the seventh day to serve as a continual reminder of His claim to our worship and the reason for it. The same creative power of God that brought our physical lives into existence is exercised to bring us new spiritual life as well. The new birth from spiritual death to eternal life requires just as much a miracle of God as does physical birth. So God uses the same sign to commemorate both types of creation. He says in Ezekiel 20:12, "'Moreover I gave them my sabbaths, as a sign between me and them, that they might know that I the Lord sanctify them'" (R.S.V.).

The first angel, by pleading for men to worship God as the Creator, draws attention to the Sabbath, which is His seal of creative power. Those who obey Him by observing His Sabbath receive His seal and demonstrate their loyalty to their Creator. By contrast, those who willfully reject God's control and choose to follow the beast receive its mark.

Space does not allow me to expand the theme of Sundaykeeping's relationship to salvation, but I have come to this firm conviction: In the Christian world the outward symbol and sign of rebellion against God's government and His law is in following what the medieval church did centuries ago—it replaced the fourth commandment, which stipulates the seventh day as the Sabbath, with a substitute day of worship. It is the fourth commandment alone that upholds the authority and the creative and re-creative power of God. Satan well knew that if he could undermine this commandment, he could more easily bring in such delusions as the evolutionary theory, which may well be the greatest single factor today in obliterating God from the minds of men and destroying the morals and standards of the people.

All through Scripture, God calls on men to worship Him as the Creator. The heathen who reduce Him to a god of wood or stone take from Him His authority as Creator. But what better is my God than theirs if He, too, is not the Creator?

The seventh-day Sabbath was designed by God in the very beginning to be a mighty, powerful memorial of His creative power. But that is not all. The ability of God to change my heart is dependent upon my belief in His supreme power. Thus it is that His re-creative power accompanies His creative power to accomplish not only the bringing of my being into existence but the changing of my heart. Remember David's prayer: "Create in me a clean heart, O God" (Ps. 51:10). Remember what Paul wrote, "If any one is in Christ, he is a new creation" (2 Cor. 5:17, R.S.V.).

Following his vision of the three angels and their messages, John writes: "And I saw what appeared to be a sea of glass mingled with fire, and those who had conquered the beast and its image and the number of its name, standing beside the sea of glass with harps of God in their hands. And they sing the song of Moses, the servant of God, and the song of the Lamb" (Rev. 15:2, 3, R.S.V.). " 'These are they who have come out of the great tribulation; they have washed their robes and made them white in the blood of the Lamb. Therefore are they before the throne of God, and serve him day and night within his temple; and he who sits upon the throne will shelter them with his presence. They shall hunger no more, neither thirst any more; the sun shall not strike them, nor any scorching heat. For the Lamb in the midst of the throne will be their shepherd, and he will guide them to springs of living water; and God will wipe away every tear from their eyes'" (chap. 7:14-17, R.S.V.).

Those who refuse the mark of the beast and the dreadful punishment that accompanies it do so not by their superior intellect, power, or virtue, but by God's grace and by their acceptance of Jesus Christ and His righteousness. They overcome "by the blood of the Lamb" and by their willingness to let Him change their lives and place on them His seal.

God wants to do this for *you!* I pray that every reader of these words will have this experience and finally live among the redeemed forever. Our future is gloriously bright when all the treasures of the universe will be open to us for study throughout eternity. As the endless years roll by we will have an ever richer and more glorious revelation of our God and of our Saviour, Jesus Christ. We owe everything to Him. Choose to serve Him now and then finally join the multitude of His faithful servants in a mighty chorus saying, "Blessing, and honour, and glory, and power, be unto him that sitteth upon the throne, and unto the Lamb for ever and ever" (chap. 5:13).

"Even so, come, Lord Jesus!" (chap. 22:20).

YOU CAN HAVE

NEW life

34 NEW LIFE GUIDES ARE YOURS FREE!

Why does God
permit suffering?

How to understand
the Bible!

Science, the Bible,
and God!

Jesus is coming.
When?

The secret of
answered prayer!

When you die.
What then?

ABSOLUTELY FREE! . . .
No present or future obligation!

Sent for one reason only

. . . TO GIVE NEW LIFE!

YES! Send me NEW LIFE GUIDES . . . FREE . . . No obligation!

Mr. Mrs. Miss_____
(Circle One)   (Please Print)

Address_____

City_____

State_____ **Zip**_____

Mail to: **NEW LIFE**
Box 55, Los Angeles, California 90053